Children's Art

The Development in Imaginative Drawing and Painting from Ages 3 to 11

Mary McInally

SOUTHGATE

ACKNOWLEDGEMENTS

My thanks go to Professor Mason, the Department of Art Education, Roehampton Institute, and also to Raywen Ford, Deputy Principal there, for their interest in the preparation of this book.

To Dr Maureen Cox of the University of York for her permission to reproduce some of her children's drawings and the description of the results of her research in connection with them.

My thanks also go to Frances Hardy, Headteacher of the Sacred Heart R.C. Primary School, Roehampton for her advice as a reader of this work.

I would also like to thank Grant Cooke for his continued support, particularly as a visiting art tutor in the Borough of Kingston-upon-Thames, and also for the use of some of his children's drawings.

I would like to record my appreciation of the co-operation and practical help given me by my assistant Gwenda Lloyd when we were working together in the nursery department of Corpus Christi Primary School in New Malden.

My special thanks go to all the children whose art work has been used in this book, and also to their teachers in the schools where some of the work was done, namely:

The Avenue Nursery School, New Malden
Christchurch C. of E. Junior School, New Malden
The Convent of the Sacred Hearts, Epsom
Corpus Christi R. C. Primary School, New Malden
Downsend Preparatory School, Leatherhead
Downsend School Lodge, Epsom
The Holy Cross Preparatory School, Kingston-upon-Thames
King Athelstan Junior School, Kingston-upon-Thames
Kingswood Preparatory School, Epsom
Our Lady Immaculate R. C. Primary School, Tolworth
Sacred Heart R. C. Primary School, Roehampton
St Martin's C. E. Junior School, Epsom
Tolworth Junior School

Copyright © text Mary McInally 2003
First published 2003 by Southgate Publishers Ltd

Southgate Publishers Ltd
The Square, Sandford, Crediton, Devon EX17 4LW

Printed and bound in Great Britain by J W Arrowsmith, Bristol.

British Library Cataloguing in Publication Data
A CIP catalogue record for this book is available from the British Library.

ISBN 1–85741–150–1

Fig. 34 on page 19 is reproduced by permission of the Design and Artists Copyright Society © Succession Picasso/DACS 2003.
Fig. 53 on page 27 is taken from *Education through Art* by Herbert Read, published by Faber & Faber and is reprinted by permission of David Higham Associates.

A drawing of a castle entrance by Catriona aged nine plus

CONTENTS

To Catriona, David and John, whose drawings and paintings appear throughout this book

Sketches of cars by David aged nine and ten years

INTRODUCTION

In inviting you to look through this collection of children's art my aim is to give some idea of what might be expected from each age group, from a child's time spent in the Nursery and then on through the Infant years and the Junior years. So the work reproduced in this book can be regarded as a visual development from three plus to eleven plus.

I feel that in order to understand and appreciate each broad band of development in a child's life, which for convenience I have placed in a progression of school years, it is really necessary to know what went before and what is to follow after. This is what I now hope to present to you. The main area I have chosen is children's imaginative drawing and painting, and my hope is that by looking at a selection of work from each peer-group a broader understanding of childhood expression and development will be gained.

It can be seen from their earliest years that while the use of language is still developing, their drawings can act as a short cut for them to express their innermost thoughts and ideas. At the same time these expressions provide a release of the young child's special vision of the world as they see and experience it. A quick sketch or a more carefully worked out drawing can at times act as a safety valve, giving expression to any surprises or fears that might suddenly come their way. Teachers and parents might discover that children's artistic expressions – ranging from the little sketch found crumpled and forgotten to the big painting done in class at school – could have more valuable information to impart to them than was previously realised.

So throughout the primary school years and beyond we should consider their art work as contributing to an essential part of young people's thought processes and their 'visual thinking' should be encouraged as an important part of their education, just as their facility with the spoken and written word develops. For these reasons the art lessons in school should always be looked on as providing an enjoyable aesthetic experience, with time allowed for worthwhile and meaningful work to be done.

The encouragement of drawing and painting has been emphasised throughout these pages, with the free development of individual skills particularly in mind. If this method of working is followed the importance of the subject will become apparent across the curriculum – as a natural part of maths and science, enhancing the skilful expression of history subjects, and adding fascinating illustrations to work in biology, and so on. But this will only happen provided that the proper balance of subjects is maintained within the school syllabus.

To help increase the teacher's awareness in dealing with the National Curriculum in Art and Design and the Foundation Stage in early education, I have made useful references throughout the text, touching on some of the programmes of study included.

Drawing of trees on a hill

LIST OF FIGURES

Unless otherwise stated, the illustrations of children's work are from my classes at Corpus Christi Primary School, New Malden or Epsom Convent School. The names David, Catriona and John refer to my own children and their work done at home.

FROM SCRIBBLES TO DRAWINGS

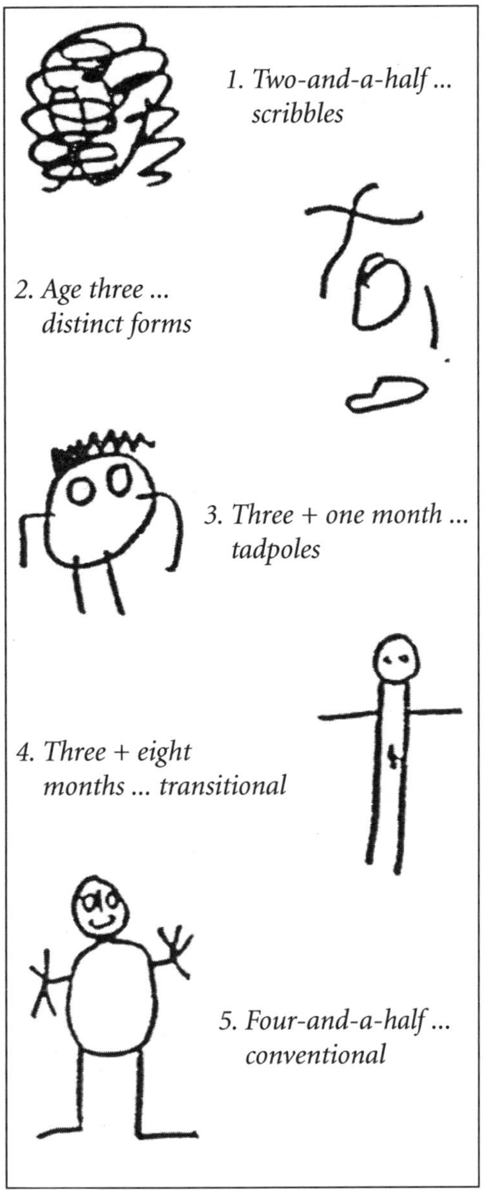

Examining children's early drawings

I will begin with the earliest months and years in the young child's development from the age of about two plus. Looking at their drawings and paintings, it can be seen that recognisable images form in the minds of human beings at a comparatively early age. The ability to express and portray these images develops fast from about the age of three onwards, and in exceptional cases as much as six months earlier. These expressions tell the observer a lot. In the months prior to this, the child is developing muscular control, is experimenting with, say, crayon or pencil and will produce what might justifiably be termed 'scribble'.

Intellectual growth

Fig. 1 shows the five average categories that Dr Maureen Cox has used to trace the time factor in this early development. She demonstrates that by the time the average child has reached the age of four-and-a-half their drawing portrays a conventional image of the human form. But children of well above average ability will often show remarkably early development in their drawings, such as in Howard's conventional-style figures in fig. 2, taken from my collection, done at the very early age of two-and-a-half, far ahead of the average child of that age. Dr Cox discusses these expressions at length in her books *Children's Drawings* (1992), *Children's Drawings of the Human Figure* (1993) and *Drawings of People by the Under-5s* (1997).

This development from scribble to more recognisable shapes indicates the state of intellectual maturity, and it can be seen that children soon develop their own personal modes of expression. The question of their individual style is discussed by Herbert Read in his book *Education Through Art* (1949), where he uses the word 'schema' to describe the images children make.

The rapidly developing pictorial expression at this stage is explained by the generally accepted estimation that half of human intellectual growth takes place somewhere between birth and four years, while another 30% develops between four and eight years. This is underlined by the fact that the average child has learnt the basic rudiments of a language in the first four years of their life.

Fig. 1. The early development of children's drawings

1. Two-and-a-half ... scribbles

2. Age three ... distinct forms

3. Three + one month ... tadpoles

4. Three + eight months ... transitional

5. Four-and-a-half ... conventional

Fig. 2. Drawing done at two-and-a-half

An example of above average ability

Following Howard's early drawing of human figures done when he was two-and-a-half, it can be seen that when just turned five he can ably manage fine details in his picture of a procession of Daleks taken from the television programme *Dr Who* (fig. 3). He shows good observation of the robots as they move relentlessly forward, and the strong pattern and texture on their metal bodies and repeated triangular outline shape all add to the drama of the scene.

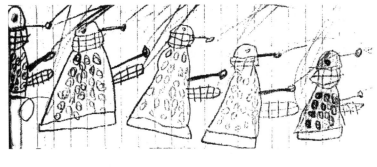

Fig. 3 Daleks moving forward

Another drawing done later by Howard at the age of five plus shows a well-proportioned police car patrolling the district (fig. 4). The handling of the drawing is well-controlled and the bold outline of the vehicle with its back window shown in convincing perspective demonstrates his ability to record realistically from memory.

A record of progress

As pictorial and verbal expression go hand-in-hand in these early years when the use of language is developing so rapidly, it is particularly helpful if the child's own description or title is noted in their own words on each drawing or painting they make at school.

It is also a valuable exercise for interested parents to preserve, date and similarly describe any pictures or sketches done by their children at home or on holiday. These items reveal a considerable amount about the outlook and development of the child, and if they are mounted on to the pages of a large scrapbook they will be of special interest in later years. The opportunity will not come again!

My suggestion would be that throughout the school years, both primary and secondary, an individual folder, containing certain key pieces of work, is kept for each pupil by the teacher. These should be carefully dated, the title given and a brief comment added about each one, so that each year's progress can be appreciated.

Useful additions can be made to these samples of work, particularly during the Nursery years, by adding the occasional print-out of a photograph of the individual child, shown either working by themselves or in a group, engaged in art and craft activities. A first-hand glimpse such as this can say a lot about the pupil – not only enlightening in its special way for the parents, but also providing useful back-up information for the teacher when making assessments for the Foundation Stage.

Fig. 4 A patrolling police-car

These folders automatically become a useful record, conveniently on hand for parents' interviews, but they should be recognised as being 'an essential requirement' rather than just an extra point of interest. The collection of work will also be an important record for any young person specialising in art subjects later on.

THE NURSERY

Fig. 5 My baby sister

Fig. 6 A clown with a string of sausages

Fig. 7 The Bluebell Railway

Looking at early expressions

Adults instinctively encourage their offspring's language ability almost from birth. Then later on, during the young child's initial experience of the Foundation Stage of their Nursery work, both teachers and parents help them to build up their reading skills and encourage their potential for learning number skills. But to a great extent it is a child's art work that reveals much about their overall development, and this singularly individual output is not always fully understood.

With this in mind, I would like to show you four examples of children's paintings done in the Nursery class (**see colour section page i**). These pieces of art work will help to clarify what I mean by 'the interpretation of children's early expressions'. They are examples of work done at about the age of four plus. On examining them, I think we would agree that plate 1 is a brilliant flight of butterflies, plate 2 is a self-portrait, plate 3 is a colourful clown and plate 4 is a birthday cake.

But look at the first painting again. The picture of the colourful clown tells me that in those early years Cathy already understood quite a lot about symmetry, rotation and the sequencing of colour and pattern when she made this painting. Katie's painting, in plate 1, reveals that she had a sure grasp of pairing of objects and lateral movement – in other words, of mathematical concepts – when she completed this.

Kathleen's self-portrait, in plate 2, portrays a little child with a well-rounded assessment of herself. She sees herself clearly as the centre of her own environment, with her blue dress, long brown hair and red shoes. Everything is in place.

The birthday cake, in plate 4, shows that this child already has a good number concept: 'I am four years old, my cake has four candles'. Rosalind shows that she understands the 'fourness of four'.

Many early pieces of art work can reveal such information if we are prepared to take a second careful look at them.

Picture-making

A world of initial experience is packed into the three or four terms the very young child spends in the Nursery class. Sonya, only just turned three, makes a typical Humpty Dumpty type of drawing to show us what her baby sister looks like (fig. 5). At three-and-a-half Leigh-Anne amusingly portrays her clown with a string of sausages (fig. 6), and Martin's train, moving along the rail of the Bluebell Railway (fig. 7), shows that at that early age he is already able to express his visual memory using precise detail.

Early learning goals

From their earliest output these young children's drawings give clear pointers as regards their aptitudes and stages of development, so we should be recognising and encouraging desirable learning outcomes among their Nursery activities at the Foundation Stage, particularly in their art work. Some four-year-olds begin to show an early feeling for perspective in their pictures, such as in Susan's drawing of a house, in which two sides of the house are drawn obliquely to the picture-plane (fig. 12). In contrast, at the same age Benjamin shows an early observation of his house from a straightforward, flat front view (fig. 10), including the door panels, letter box and smoking chimney.

An awareness of a wider world in the historical sense is already indicated by John, with his drawing of the bandaged head of an Egyptian mummy (fig. 8). Cheerful facial expressions are portrayed in the portraits of a mother cat and kitten by Laura (fig. 9), while a character study of the figures of Dorothy and Toto, from *The Wizard of Oz*, is offered by Joseph (fig. 13). The frightening aspect of a crocodile's head is quite dramatically shown in a line drawing by Samuel (fig. 11), and Ben's drawing of a submarine demonstrates future promise of technical ability in its accurate observation and detail (fig. 14).

Fig. 8 An Egyptian mummy

Fig. 9 Mother cat and kitten

Fig. 10 My house

Fig. 11 A crocodile's head

Above: Fig. 12 Susan's house
Left: Fig. 13 Dorothy and Toto

Fig. 14 A submarine

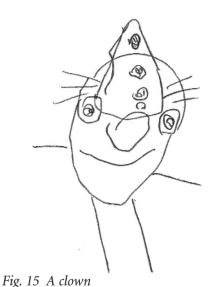

Fig. 15 A clown

Fig. 16 A lady

Fig. 17 A drawing of himself by Alec

Rapidly changing stages of development

In their early drawings of the human figure young children make rapid progress, moving forward from one concept to another. In James' clown (fig. 15), drawn when he was three plus, we have a drawing which is little more than an enlarged head and body merged into one shape with stick arms and legs. The clown's face is remarkably amusing and expressive, and the child expresses the whole image in one shape.

In her drawing done at the age of four plus, which she calls 'A Lady' (fig. 16), Eun Soo makes use of a neck to join the head on to the body. Her main interest has been to show a lady's face, which she has done well. In the rest of the drawing we have the typical concept of arms sticking out at each side of the body, with no hands. Directly at the bottom of this body shape are two small feet.

Some young children's drawings progress fast but they nevertheless still have a 'jointed' look, with the arms, legs and head added as separate units. Alec, aged four years seven months, uses the device of a short curved line to show his shoulders, which link his arms to his body (fig. 17). These 'segmented' figures are gradually replaced between the ages of five and seven, although occasionally a whole outline figure is expressed earlier, at about the age of four, as in Kathleen's 'Myself' (plate 2).

Making their own choices

Very young children will produce an unending variety of ideas in their art work if they are given the freedom of making their own choices. The danger is that some teachers may not allow this freedom of expression simply because they do not appreciate the children's capabilities. For the same reason the tendency might be to prescribe one set subject, where all the children paint the same thing that day. The result of this can be seen in many wall displays where a set of almost identical pictures has been produced by the class. Under such circumstances children tend to copy from each other as it seems to them that this similarity is what is expected by the teacher. Such problems can be overcome through good in-service instruction where it is shown that widely individual expressions can be made even within set projects.

Examples of self-expression

Let us look at four paintings (**see colour section page ii**). In plate 8 there is a delightfully fresh sense of pattern in Angela's 'Teacup and plate with cakes', typical of a child bringing to school an image of something seen recently at home. Darren's 'A fierce black snake' (plate 7) demonstrates the ability of a young child to make a startling portrayal of the dangerous creature he may have seen either on television or in a book. In plate 5 Joanna's picture of 'A village with a pond' shows an unusual grouping of buildings at an age when young children mostly like to paint single objects. Finally, Ben's very colourful 'A fire engine' (plate 6) is done in such a well-recognised silhouette that the fire bell can almost be heard jangling.

This is the range of images and modes of self-expression we should be looking for and expecting to find at this age. The doors should always be open to opportunities for children to make such interesting and worthwhile pictures as the ideas come flooding into their minds.

Providing the right equipment

There is still a widespread misconception that young children should only be given large paintbrushes and giant crayons to work with. They can use these very well, but brushes and crayons also need to be graded for them, from fine to large, simply because small hands need the opportunity to do fine work as well as bold, so finer types of brush should be available for them to use as well as the large hog hair ones. The same rule applies to pens and pencils, and fresh bright paints, creamy in consistency, should always be ready for use. The difference in quality of the work produced by children with access to a good choice of art materials is marked.

Making a start

When they are first introduced to painting young children love to experiment with random brush strokes. But the time comes when the suggestion that they should now paint 'something' needs to be made. A very successful teaching strategy to employ at this level is to discuss the child's undertaking with them and to make suggestions while they are working. Children love to chat about what they are doing and conversation with adults seems to stimulate and encourage them, and often helps to fill out their ideas. It is a good idea to enlist extra help for this purpose, through a parent rota, for instance. This discussion links in well with their all-important language development as well as helping with practical matters – such as preventing a brush laden with black paint being put in the white pot!

The capabilities of young children

I feel that today in early education our young children are still not given sufficient opportunity to develop their drawing and painting as part of their all-round training. This means that standards in creative art work tend to fall behind from the beginning, and there may be a lapse of a year or two before any useful instructions are given in the subject. Hence the words of the American educationalist, Elliot W. Eisner, 'If we have erred in the general theories we have developed, and therefore in the schools, I believe it has been in underestimating what children are capable of learning. Education in the visual arts has been no exception.' (Elliot W. Eisner, *Cognition and Curriculum*, 1982, p.70).

RECEPTION

Picture-making

I n the content of their pictures Reception children have now come a long way in their development from the early years. Their people are still mainly looking straight at us, but profile views are used as well for people in cars, soldiers on horseback, babies in prams, animals and so on. The stick arms and legs are gone and limbs are expressed as separate units, with hands not always drawn in. Personalities are depicted with their own special clothes, rosy cheeks and facial expressions; an example is the character study 'My Daddy', noticeably wearing a brown tie, which was drawn by David at five years ten months (fig. 18). In outdoor pictures there is now more detail added, such as the sky shown as a blue strip above, and objects are sometimes shown larger in the foreground and smaller in the background, like the spade in Rachel's 'At the seaside' (fig. 19), done at five plus.

A great deal of movement and energy can be expressed in children's work at this stage. Ian's picture of himself playing football, at the age of four years eleven months, is typical of this lively expression as he draws himself with a smiling face, jumping in the air and kicking the ball. His surroundings are depicted with the sun shining above and green grass underfoot and for good measure he details the studs on his football boots!

Personal devices

A lot that is portrayed in their picture-making shows that Reception children are constantly widening their horizons and keenly observing the world around them. Some begin to work out personal devices to enable them to express their more complex ideas on paper. They use these 'contrived' drawings to create some form of order in their own minds concerning their latest discoveries. Such representations need to be appreciated and understood by the teacher, and their meanings and intentions interpreted and discussed with the child.

'Folding-over' and 'layering'

A typical device used at this age is the 'fold-over' drawing where both sides of an image are shown at once, on an imaginary axis. This can be seen in a picture entitled 'A cart being drawn across the sand' by David, aged four years seven months (fig. 23). Here his horse's head is shown 'head-on' with both sides presented at the same time, by using a flattened-out view. Picasso used this exaggerated vision in rather the same way in his Cubist Period when he made his painting in 1937 of *The*

Fig. 18 My Daddy

Fig. 19 At the seaside

Fig. 20 Ian playing football

Weeping Woman now in the Tate Modern. Catriona chooses to show a typical 'fold-over' view of cars moving in a half-circle, in her street scene (fig. 22). This was drawn at the age of five years ten months, and in this case she makes use of the device of flattening out the image she represents round a central axis.

In fig. 21 we see a picture by David aged four years eight months, in which traffic is shown moving along a busy highway jammed with cars and lorries. There is even a transporter carrying more cars on top of it! To express his view of the road always lengthening out away from him into the distance, he uses the device here of showing a variety of vehicles continuing along it by 'layering' a series of drawings one on top of the other.

Fig. 21 A transporter carrying cars

Children's art as a springboard for adult artists

While considering these early stages of children's art it is interesting to note how the work produced by children has been an inspiration to many major twentieth-century artists. In his book *The Innocent Eye: Children's Art and the Modern Artist* (1997) Jonathan Fineberg reveals how dependent many modern artists have been on children's art. These include Vassily Kandinsky, an early pioneer in abstract painting, whose ideas Fineberg suggests were at times drawn from particular pictures in a collection of children's work. He shows how Paul Klee found stimulus in examples of his own early drawings, and describes how the energy and exhilaration in Juan Miro's work is paralleled in the carefully documented work of his daughter Dolores, that he kept from her earliest childhood. He also observes how Picasso's style is at times indebted to the swift, impulsive simplicity he saw in his own children's pictures, which he studied with enormous delight.

Fig. 22 Street scene

Fig. 23 A cart being drawn across the sand

Fig. 24 A boy today and some months ago

Fig. 25 A lighthouse

Fig. 26 Fruit

Perspective and time

At the age of five years three months Catriona makes use of 'the dawn of perspective' that can develop in a child's mind at about this time. She links it in this case with a sense of time by pointing out that the figure in the foreground of her picture represents 'a boy today' while the one in the background is 'as he was some months ago' (fig. 24). An adult surrealist painter such as Salvador Dali will often use the same device in a landscape to denote the passing of time.

Another point of interest in this picture is the use she makes of a variety of fairly intricate patterns to decorate the boy's shirt. She obviously enjoys picking out the pattern-strips in different colours and her ideas here may have been stimulated by work done in school. The figures still face forward and the facial features are presented simply, but the child's interests centre on the use of pattern and colour, coupled with the realisation and portrayal of the passing of time.

Drawing and painting from models

The large painting filling the page with bright colour is a priority, not just at this stage, but throughout the primary school, and children will draw upon their own mental images to carry out this work to a great extent. However, it is not too early at four plus to get them to observe and draw from models, such as well-designed toys, or from natural objects, such as fruit and flowers, or from pictures and photographs, because such an exercise helps them to learn what these things look like, how they are made, or even how they work.

In this way children can build up a personal visual vocabulary that will stay with them. Making sketches helps them to 'feel round' a structure and this will later be of assistance in 3D work. The examples shown here are by Sarah at four plus, whose lighthouse picture was done after making a drawing from a photograph (fig. 25), and a child of five plus in a Japanese school, who has used pen-and-wash for a picture of fruit.

Tiffany, just turned five, makes use of a photograph for her picture of a hedgehog among the autumn leaves (fig. 27, opposite). Her drawing shows she can successfully combine lively creativity and imagination with an ability to use correctly observed detail.

Equipment

Pencils and pens should always be available on the paint table alongside the brushes because even though a child will often paint directly with a brush, the opportunity to draw first should always be there. Each child should also have their own A4 sketchbook available to put down any thoughts and ideas through their drawings. The contents may be revealing and make a valuable record of progress, particularly if the pages are dated and the subject matter briefly described.

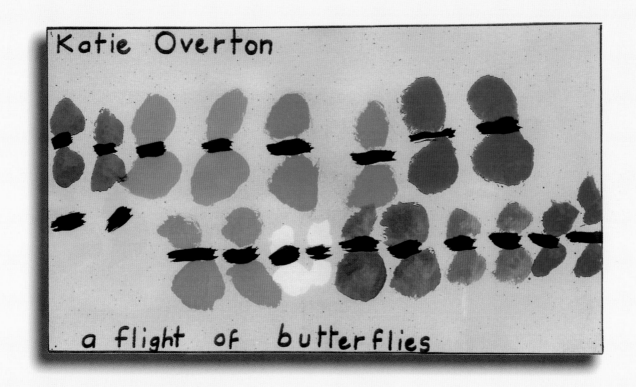

Top: *Plate 1 A flight of butterflies*
Above: *Plate 2 Myself*
Above right: *Plate 3 A circus clown*
Right: *Plate 4 My birthday cake with four candles*

Left: *Plate 5 A village with a pond*
Below: *Plate 6 A fire engine*

Left: *Plate 7 A fierce black snake*
Below: *Plate 8 A teacup and plate with cakes*

Above: *Plate 9 Firework pattern by Rachela*
Left: *Plate 10 Flowers by Helen*
Below left: *Plate 11 A writing pattern*
Below: *Plate 12 Block-print pattern by Marco*

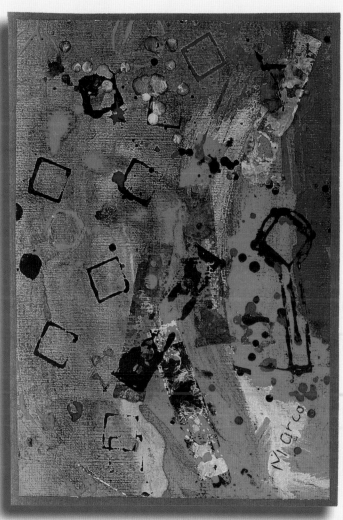

"Mother smacking Susan".
Picture full of strong movement.
Diagonal patterns on
both dresses accentuate
movement.

SUSAN

Top left: *Plate 13 Mother smacking Susan*
Top right: *Plate 14 Decorative roundel*
Above: *Plate 15 Potato and plasticine print*
Left: *Plate 16 A dragon*

Textiles

In Key Stage 1 children begin to combine their skills in art and design when working practically and imaginatively with textiles. This work is important for early hand-to-eye co-ordination development and in the Reception year children should be confidently able to manage several types of simple stitches in producing creative collage work. Michelle's work, at five plus, shows her originality in the use of felt and canvas (fig. 28). Here she uses blanket stitch and adds shiny buttons.

Fig. 27 My hedgehog

Timothy, at five plus, shows his obvious enjoyment of stitching in lines and textures to give character to his wooden railway truck in fig. 29. The wheels give the impression of the heavy vehicle trundling along the curving track. Too often young children's experience is restricted to the use of sewing cards, which curtail their creativity when they could be using a needle and thread freely from an early age. Techniques of weaving can also be explored using simple card looms and experimenting with a variety of coloured threads, wools and yarns.

A developing use of pattern, texture and colour

Reception children should now be able to cut out and stick reliably without too much help. They should also be able to work as a group to create a frieze or make a window display. An example is shown on page 18 (fig. 31), where large butterflies and flowers have been made from children's folded cut-outs and painted and pasted shapes added. An introduction to such skills and the use of such simple symmetrical concepts naturally paves the way for later work within the framework of the National Curriculum by building up children's knowledge and understanding of the subject at this early Foundation Stage.

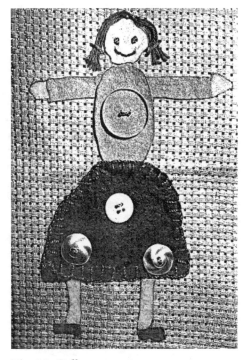

Fig. 28 Collage

Pattern-making
Pattern-making can play a role through simple block-printing. At this stage writing patterns are especially important to help with the learning of good handwriting. This should follow the rule of frequently working large, using brush or crayon in a free manner to encourage experiment, rhythm and flow.

Wax-resist
Children benefit by seeing the results of taking their work a stage further. In plates 9 and 10 (page iii) this has been done by the use of the process of wax-resist. Rachela and Helen, both turned five, first coloured in their patterns with a bold use of their wax crayons. They then brushed over a wash of black to bring out the colours in an exciting contrast.

Block-printing and colour mixing
To make the lively pattern in plate 12 (page iii) Marco, four-and-a-half,

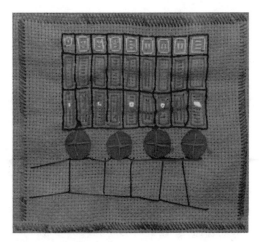

Fig. 29 Coal truck

Fig. 30 The three kings and
The three bears

first painted several colours freely on a sheet of wallpaper. He then experimented with some block-printing and finished by dropping spots of paint over it in different colours. The mixing of primary colours can also be investigated in this way and exciting discoveries made – so no prescriptive teaching methods are necessary at this stage since the curriculum requirements are being more than adequately covered!

Expressing mathematical concepts

The two pictures in fig. 30 show that Reception children at five plus are able to express their ideas well using mathematical concepts as a matter of course. In 'The three kings' Anne's kings wear tall crowns and one of them is shown as dark skinned. 'The three bears' shows that Paul understands 'the threeness of three' and he provides a scale of sizes as well, from the tall father bear down to a small fat baby! He includes an outline of the table and the three chairs for good measure.

Fig. 31 Display of children's butterflies on
a classroom window

Manual dexterity and 3D art

Children's manual dexterity needs to be encouraged. This can be done through handling clay, cutting and sticking paper and card, block-printing and bubble-printing, or by making dough into toy food and baking and painting their objects.

Children particularly enjoy expressing their imaginative ideas through junk-modelling. This activity gives them an exciting experience of the three-dimensional work that will play such an important part throughout the future programmes of the National Curriculum. At this stage they should be encouraged to tackle fairly simple shapes and some help will be needed at times with cutting and fixing to avoid disappointment with the final results. This way of 'assisted working' in the initial stages becomes a positive step forward in the children's training in handling constructional craft work, and the final results are rewarding.

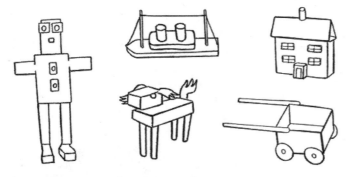

Fig. 32 Some examples of 3D art done
in Reception

YEAR 1

Work progresses to Key Stage 1 this year so the National Curriculum programme continues to provide the progressive framework for teaching art and design throughout the school that was embarked on at the Foundation Stage in the Nursery. Children starting in the Nursery may be well ahead in their art work by the time they reach Infant level, having covered many of the rudiments of their Key Stage 1 work well in advance of what is required of them by the time they reach Years 1 and 2.

Exploring the work of artists

At this age children enjoy looking at drawings and paintings by some adult artists, particularly in relation to their own work, and they should be able to give their reasons for liking or not liking a particular work of art. In this way an artist's picture can become an adventurous departure point to be explored further. The teacher can suggest that they try out something similar in their own paintings and apply their own ideas to what they have seen, using a variety of colours, shapes and textures to create their own pictures.

Fig. 33 Aaron's garden with sunflowers

The hope is that when children look at the designs and techniques of others, some of the visual influences of these beautiful and interesting things will 'rub off' and help their own work. Although they mostly learn through individual experience, they can also be encouraged 'to leap beyond their own boundaries' by looking at examples of art and design that show different ways of portraying similar subjects to their own.

Keith Gentle makes this very relevant comment in his book *Teaching Painting in the Primary School* (page 81): 'Once the sharing of work by artists, craftworkers and designers has started, teachers will soon find their knowledge and understanding is increased and will enjoy sharing this with children.'

After looking at Gustav Klimt's *Country Garden with Sunflowers*, some Year 1 children painted pictures giving their interpretations of what they had seen. In his painting done at the age of six years nine months, Aaron used a variety of forms and textures in exciting colours and lively brushwork to describe his own impression of the picture.

It is useful if the teacher makes up a notebook with examples of drawings and paintings by the artists that children particularly relate to at different stages. Young people are naturally interested in pictures of other children and among my choices would be Picasso's portrait of his son Paul. Painted with a clarity and almost childlike simplicity of style, it is readily accessible to children.

Fig. 34 Portrait of Paul, the Artist's son

Opportunities to express themselves

While we are considering these different ways of working there are certain fundamentals we must be careful to keep in mind with regard to giving children space to express themselves in their own right. Some of these essentials are expertly summed up in the introduction of *Art in the early years of schooling*, edited by Margaret Morgan: 'What of our children?' she asks. 'Their personal symbolism is based on the very stuff of living – their hopes, imaginings and fears – themselves portrayed in many ways. Friends and enemies, family pets, possessions, homes and gardens. Beautiful things are celebrated, wars and horrors are played out, reality, imagination and fantasy interrelate. Colours, shapes and patterns are enjoyed for their own intrinsic qualities.' I hope you will find an abundance of what she describes throughout this book!

Observing and interpreting the wider world

This picture of a tree in autumn losing its leaves is part of an autumn project done in Year 1. The angle of the branches and the colours show Isabelle's ability, at the age of six, to observe and interpret what she sees happening in the world about her.

When children are in the Nursery and Reception classes they tend to be little individuals who still identify closely with their home backgrounds, but the Year 1 child identifies more fully with both school and school activities by making special friends and merging in socially with larger groups in the playground.

Fig. 35 A tree in autumn

X-ray pictures

In all age groups there is an overlap in children's modes of expression in their art work and some still employ special devices to show something they want to express. An example is the X-ray picture, which looks through things and tells the viewer what is going on inside. So it is not surprising that Catriona, as a Year 1 child at five years nine months, wanting to show the workings of the inside of her school, uses the device of simply removing the front wall to produce an X-ray picture of a section of the building on two levels, with little figures climbing up and down stairs, sitting at their desks or moving along the corridors.

Fig. 36 Inside my school

Missing parts

From the earliest age, some children will, either by accident or by design, leave out one detail in their picture as they add another. Hands or even arms might be missing on one or more of the figures in a group, and this may occur even when the child has included them in earlier pictures. It seems that this is either because the child forgets to put a detail in when they are busily working, or because they are satisfied with the drawing as it is and they may simply have no wish to include anything further.

Awareness of detail

Faces now show more expression, and may smile, scowl or show fear. Hands with pairs of lines drawn round the fingers are used. Eyelashes and teeth appear and eyes have pupils instead of being completely filled in with one colour. These are all clearly shown in 'The Baby Jesus', drawn by John at the age of six (fig. 37). People are now shown in groups, and a greater awareness of gender differences in boys' and girls' clothes is evident, as well as in girls' hairstyles. There is a greater use of pattern and textures, such as on a dragon's scaly back, painted by Giselle at six plus (plate 16, page iv). All this shows an increased ability to control media, and the conscious use of varying techniques.

Fig. 37 The baby Jesus

Pattern-making

By now there should be no difficulty for the majority of children to attain their National Curriculum targets satisfactorily in imaginative picture-making and pattern-making.

Writing patterns used freely, as an extension of children's writing pattern exercises, can be colourful and attractive. The children like making freely painted, patterned roundels with strong radiating shapes, midway between writing patterns and free, imaginative design (see Ben's pattern, drawn at six plus, in plate 14, page iv).

Children should take longer to complete a piece of work now because their experience enables them to see the possibility of taking it further. This is particularly true with their pattern-making and craft-work, such as block-printing. They often want to tackle a second stage in their work and continue it in another lesson – for instance, by overprinting a second colour over the first, as in plate 15 (page iv).

Examples of one child's work at this stage: Catriona

Children will begin to use a lot of 'imagery' at this stage to express some of the day-to-day experiences of their lives. In fig. 38 Catriona is

Fig. 38 My friends at school

Fig. 39 Blind girl

Fig. 40 A naughty dirty girl

Fig. 41 A lady in a coffin

making just such an observation in a drawing of two of her friends being met outside school by their mother and young brother. The figures are predictably facing forward and she uses the same X-ray device as before (fig. 36) to show the boy's teddy bear dropped down inside his pram, which has its four wheels drawn almost in one straight line. But interestingly enough, at this age of six years two months, she has made a noticeable advance on her earlier drawings by employing her visual perception in the obvious use of 'occlusion', setting the figure of her friend Jill partly in front of the mother and so obscuring some of the mother's dress and the whole length of her right leg.

Considerable interest is also shown by Catriona in the girls' uniform dresses, cardigans and hats and the establishment of their names and the young brother's name and age, which she has written in. This interest in clothes coincided with her cutting out and dressing up paper figures.

A feeling for drama

Children will sometimes feel the need to make quite a dramatic drawing in order to convey the image of something they have seen or heard about that may have shocked or worried them. Or it may be because they have suddenly come to realise the reality of something they had not fully understood before.

Three such expressions were made by Catriona at the age of six years three months, which convey this need to portray something startling or different to the viewer. In fig. 39 she makes a poignant observation entitled 'Blind girl'. In fig. 40 she shows her strong feelings about 'A naughty dirty girl', who does not match her concept of a clean and orderly existence! In the same month she made use of her X-ray technique to show her realisation one day of what she termed 'A lady in a coffin', after seeing a funeral procession (fig. 41).

Development in content and style

The picture-making of the Year 1 child reflects a distinct advance in both content and style. Figures now show movement and are viewed in profile as well as frontally, as in Catriona's picture 'Mother smacking Susan', done at age six years four months (plate 13, page iv). The drawing is full of strong action, accentuated by the diagonal pattern on both mother's and child's dresses. It should be noted that the mother's hands and some facial features are missing, while the figure of Susan is complete except for the hands.

Two months later, at the age of six-and-a-half, in a very detailed picture called 'Skipping' (fig. 42), Catriona chooses to draw the hands of the two children shown standing in profile turning the rope, but the hands of the third child jumping over the rope are missing. This last picture was made during a period of considerable expansion in her visual expression, as testified by the fact that the body parts are now integrated, and she has started drawing in necks on her figures, whose arms bend, and knees also appear. Additionally, she shows a great deal

Fig. 42 Skipping

of interest in the patterns on the clothes of her two main figures and their hats and hairstyles. So either she may have made a conscious decision not to devote any more time to the third figure, through lack of interest, or her recall of her cognitive image of the scene may have faded and thus the third figure is left incomplete.

An overview of work done in Year 1

A further look over the work done this year shows how the children's pictorial images and pattern designs have advanced in that time-span. It is noticeable that these children now control their work well and are interested in taking their designs and paintings a stage or two forward by making use of added colour and texture. (The three pictures referred to here are on page iv.)

For instance, Giselle's painting of a dragon (plate 16) makes use of the lines and curves of the dragon's body in a very positive way and the textures representing the creature's scales follow interestingly round the shape. These are typical skills which begin to occur in Year 1.

Ben makes use of a zigzag writing pattern and a freely conceived flower shape to make his roundel (plate 14). The work is taken further by developing the lines of the flower over colour applied earlier and by adding textures to the centre.

Rachel's block-print (plate 15) shows three stages in her work. She uses red paint to sponge the paper in preparation for doing a potato-print. The print is then applied in a regular drop-pattern. She finally makes a rolled plasticine shape and experiments freely by using it for over-printing. This gives her work an exciting contrasting texture.

Fig. 43 Hadrian's Wall

Fig. 44 Taking baby for a walk

Fig. 45 Mummy shopping

As all teachers well know, general assessments and record-keeping play a large part in monitoring the work of Year 2, but if my suggestions here are followed, the expectations in Art should be more than adequately covered throughout the normal year's work.

The local environment

In line with the broad cultural requirements of the National Curriculum Programme of Study in Key Stage 1, children should begin to show an awareness of their environment, and this growing familiarity should now be reflected in their drawings. Different types of houses (old and new) should be appearing in their work, as well as shops and other buildings seen in the district they live in. Their vision will broaden out and they will include street scenes, the local park, countryside, seascapes, etc. in their pictures. This aspect of their developing expression can be encouraged in an illustrative way if used to accompany written descriptions.

In fig. 44 Laura, aged six plus, has made a drawing of herself pushing a pram in her local park, to go with her story 'Taking baby for a walk', while in fig. 43, David, just turned seven, shows an interesting end view of Hadrian's Wall under attack, after making a holiday visit.

A variety of cultures

This growing awareness in young children of their wider surroundings should help them begin to build up an appreciation of their own rich heritage. At the same time, living in a multicultural society and with access to excellent school programmes and television documentaries, they should also begin to enjoy and appreciate learning about a variety of cultures existing in the world. These themes will be explored further in the chapters about Key Stage 2 work.

The use of occlusion

The rate of cognitive development is still rapid in children at this stage and the art work of the Year 2 child begins to show a maturity hitherto missing in their picture-making. Blue skies have moved down to the horizon, clouds begin to make an appearance, and trees and flowers are less symbolic in their shape. Animals and people tend to be shown in groups rather than standing in line as before, and occlusion occurs, with one thing being drawn in front of another, partially obscuring objects behind. The herd of rhinoceros in a picture carried out in pen and pastel by John at the age of seven years two months is a good example of this. Here the vision of the grassland and sky is generally more mature, the animals are viewed more flexibly from varying angles, and movement is shown among the herd (plate 17, page v).

Development of a more conventional approach

Because children are now better able to produce something recognisable in the conventional sense, the contrived drawings of the younger child, such as the X-ray pictures or fold-over perspective, have mostly disappeared. People are depicted more often as characters in drawings made from both imagination and observation, and figures are 'contoured' instead of having their limbs separately attached. Men may now sport a moustache and wear spectacles or waistcoat, and the woman in 'Mummy shopping' is well observed by David at seven plus (fig. 45), with cropped hair, necklace and wearing a hat. In a picture entitled 'Teacher and iron', drawn from observation with the teacher acting as a model, arms are no longer depicted in one straight line but they bend and the hand grips the handle of the electric iron the man is using (fig. 46).

Fig. 46 *Teacher and iron*

Observation and imaginative work

Drawing from observation now comes into its own and the child begins to portray the immediate world around them, as in Clare's drawing, at the age of six plus, of Sarah's bike (fig. 47), rich in technical observation. More detail also crowds into the children's creative pictures, and their work now displays a deepening imagination in portraying their fantasies. This is linked to their increasing ability to record in more detail what they have seen – such as Robert's dumper-truck ready to empty its load (fig. 48). With a growing interest in his environment, Robert draws a sizeable truck loaded high with soil. The scale of the powerful vehicle is shown against the simple outline of a rather small-looking man on the far side.

Fig. 47 *Sarah's bike*

Children's widening skills and developing general ability in their everyday lives, both at home and in school, are now becoming evident in their imaginative drawings. At seven years six months, Catriona makes a surprisingly interesting drawing of how she sees her friend looking at herself in the mirror. The drawing shows matching detail in the clothes and the hair. To complete the effect the facial expressions are carefully matched as well.

Fig. 48
A dumper truck

Fig. 49 *Looking in the mirror*

Three-dimensional work

The Year 2 child already well used to the feel of clay will have made simple pot shapes and done modelling in previous classes. As they now begin to show their ability to draw people and animals in a more conventional style, so their modelling will correspond in both shape and texture. In their art and design it is desirable for them to gain three-dimensional experience and modelling is one obvious choice.

Fig. 50 Examples of children's pottery and modelling

Textiles

In their textile work the children can now use coloured felts to make something useful and decorative, such as a toy or a pincushion that can be stuffed. This involves the tasks of planning, designing and then transferring their ideas into a finished piece of work. Simple flat shapes can be used, such as a ladybird, butterfly, fish or flower. Amanda's design for a decorative fish (fig. 51) followed these simple lines.

By the end of Key Stage 1 children should be working practically and imaginatively with such a wide range of materials that suitable strategies can be employed to encourage their responses to the visual elements in the world around them. An example of this was an activity in which children investigated the designs and colours in printed textiles and the variety of shapes in a collection of buttons. Using the examples they had seen as a starting point, they then recorded their responses by using free visual expression. The results can be seen in the examples of fabric design in plates 18 and 19 (on page v), and in the large 'Buttons and cloth' wall display (fig. 52).

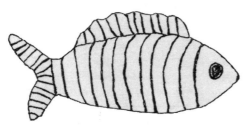

Fig. 51 A toy fish

In plate 19 Danielle, aged seven years two months, creates a trellis structure similar to the upholstery pattern she has seen. Keeping the regularity of the original pattern, she makes adventurous and experimental use of colour. In plate 18 Gary, at seven years ten months, is interested in an all-over flower pattern. He adds to his ideas by introducing bold highlights and also varies the tones and textures as part of his own expression.

The classroom display showed the children responding individually to the patterns and colours in the variety of fabrics they had seen, and making links with their own work. Their large drawings of buttons also gave them the opportunity to express their ideas visually about the shapes and designs they had examined.

Fig. 52 A classroom wall display

At first sight the programme of work in art and design in Key Stage 2 covering the junior years may seem quite demanding, but whatever is to be achieved in the four years ahead is simply a development and consolidation of what was begun in the nursery and infant school previously and which in its turn will go forward into the secondary years. Much of the problem lies in the lack of lesson time available, but a lot can be done if art work is incorporated across the curriculum, in such subjects as history or natural science, where work could be done on a large scale for a wall frieze, for instance. In addition, a lot of design work can take place in the course of maths teaching.

Moving towards visual realism

In their self-expression children at this age may be at what might be called 'a halfway-house'. On the one hand, the quality of work can still show a charming, childlike expression, as in Mark's 'My brother and I' (plate 21, page vi), drawn in crayon from memory and imagination. But at the same time there is a developing ability to begin to draw things as they are seen, as visual realism takes over. This ability to draw in a more realistic sense should be encouraged and nurtured if work is to progress and the transition to further developmental stages is to occur naturally. An example of this development can be seen in Marjorie's self-portrait (fig. 53). Both drawings were done at age seven plus.

Fig. 53 A self-portrait

Grant Cooke, the Art tutor on the Brycbox Team, when it was part of the Art Advisory Service in Kingston-upon-Thames, brought out a booklet in 1982, entitled *Reach towards Realism*, dealing with the introduction of children to some of the basic drawing conventions. In it he said, 'I believe one of the aims of a teacher concerned with children's visual education should be to give children some experience of drawing from direct observation. This helps them to learn that they can develop skills which will enable them to create images of things which they will have directly experienced visually, and make these images believable.'

If this essential training is not given, children's progress is checked and they often start doing what is termed 'clever drawing'. Their typical output becomes a facility for making the cartoon-type figures that appear in the language of the graffiti artist. These drawings are crude and far from clever, and should not be encouraged.

Fig. 54 Shoes

Drawing and sketching objects

Opportunity should be given for straightforward object drawing, such as 'Shoes', by Nicola and Jennifer, both seven plus, and Stephen, eight plus, (fig. 54) in order to foster the ability to draw well, and to continue to make progress in realistic drawing. Single objects or still-life groups can be used, also portraits of friends or a pet animal. Outdoor sketching should be done, including drawings of houses, churches, the school car park, trees, etc. These opportunities should be provided to develop the child artist's drawing skills.

We saw earlier how in the Reception class the practice of encouraging children to draw from objects, pictures or photographs will build up their visual vocabulary in the early years. If this is encouraged throughout the infant years, the transition towards a more mature visual expression will occur naturally. In my opinion not enough is expected from children in the visual arts during the primary school years. I feel this is a problem that would best be solved by the use of specialist help and advice being given by the head of the art department, at least from the top infant level, and followed up throughout the primary school by means of good in-service training.

The resource area

A collection of interesting things housed in the resource area will automatically become a useful back-up and will increase the children's interest in natural and made objects. Kate's sensitive drawing of a shell, done when she was seven plus, is an example of how this stimulus works.

Classroom organisation

In schools where classrooms are used for art, the space can be made more suitable for this work by adapting pairs of desks into convenient worktables simply by laying lightweight boards over them. Another alternative is to move the desks to the sides of the room and to cover the floor with newspapers. The children then work on the floor round the perimeter, leaving a convenient space in the centre.

Fig. 55 Spider shell

Care of equipment

It is important to have paints properly mixed, brushes clean and pencils and charcoal ready before work begins. The best way of managing powder paints is by using square biscuit tins to hold nine 'baked bean' tins for the colours, to be shared between two children with two brushes in each of the round tins. The tins are secure for handling and won't spill. If the paints are stirred regularly and water is added, they will last throughout the term; they can then be thrown out and easily replaced. Mixing colours should be well established by now – enamel or plastic plates will serve as a palette.

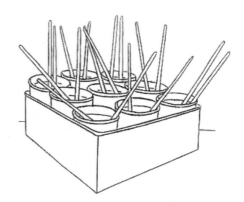

Junior picture-making

To start the lesson a discussion about a selection of subjects should take place among the whole group, with the use of visual aids to stimulate ideas. Themes such as 'The Circus' or 'At the Seaside' are popular, according to the time of year. Alternatively, the National Curriculum programme or a school project may be used. Reminders should be given to the children about filling the page satisfactorily, not working too small, and not having everything in a row at the bottom of the page! When drawings are completed, using a soft pencil or charcoal, and painting is ready to begin, further instructions should be given about filling in large areas with colour first. If this is not impressed on them, children will naturally start by painting all the small bits that interest them. Backgrounds and foregrounds should be scrubbed in with large brushes or sponged in initially to cover large areas. More colour and texture will be added at a later stage as the work progresses.

Mutual encouragement

Under these large-group working conditions children act as a catalyst for each other and the excitement builds up as they talk about their work. After break-time the children will come back with a 'fresh eye' for their work. This is a good time for the teacher to hold up any specially promising examples and note that this or that is 'what we are aiming for'. Children are interested in each other's pictures and time spent on discussing them is not only valuable, but is also fulfilling the requirements of the National Curriculum by encouraging self-appraisal and providing an opportunity to appreciate and learn from other children's work.

Different cultures and times: a study of textiles and other media

The decoration of pottery and other domestic utensils, in styles handed down through the centuries by North American Indian people, provides a wealth of examples of strong geometric patterns. Their woven cloth, rug-making and basketry, using natural fibres in the earliest times, and later mixtures of cotton and wool with the added use of beadwork, makes an absorbing study for this age group.

Through their own previous work with textiles and pottery, children can make connections with the Indian methods of print-making, weaving and hand-made ceramics, and they take delight in the animal motifs, such as bison and giant eagle, used by these people in their decorative work. The impression made on James from looking at the work of Indian craftspeople is clearly seen in his own striking eagle design (plate 22, page vi).

Fig. 56 An Indian tepee

There are opportunities for working in groups when children are engaged on such topics as making Viking boats, a Roman aqueduct, a medieval castle or an Indian settlement with tepees (fig. 56).

Developing appropriate vocabulary

Suitable materials for both large-scale and small-scale work should always be on hand and children will extend their vocabulary as they talk about their work. They now begin to describe such things as 'a fine or heavy line', 'bright or pale colour', 'rough or fine texture' and 'foreground, background, horizon'. Pauline uses 'a fine pen line' in her drawing of freesias (fig. 58). This descriptive use of words is a valuable language source.

Getting the balance right

When asked about the place of art and general subjects in education, in a recent radio discussion programme, Ken Robinson, Professor of Arts Education at the University of Warwick, put the answer succinctly. He said, 'I don't think it is a matter of deciding which is more or less important. Primary education is certainly to give children the skills they need to go on to further work in secondary education and beyond. But it is also to find out what their own strengths and weaknesses are, what their talents and abilities are, and it is to provide them with a foundation for all their later learning. I think it is important not to see it as a contest between literacy and numeracy and other things.' He continued, 'Art and music develop very important aspects of children's intelligence. Of their capacity to handle feelings.

Fig. 57 Fighting ships

Of their ability to communicate with other people their cultural understanding and social values. Literacy and numeracy aren't at odds with these things – they are as important, and I am keen to argue the case that it is not a choice between them. It is getting the balance right.'

Time given to art

The proportion of time given to art needs to be considered in this respect. Care should be taken in the junior school that a fair proportion of time is allowed for art and design. What percentage of time, for instance, during the week does it have compared with that devoted to written work and maths? Teachers will find lunchtime clubs one good way of solving the problem of finding extra time without causing undue pressure in other directions. Ways should also be sought to maintain the balance by using art and design work in conjunction with general subjects.

Fig. 58 A drawing of freesias

Links with other areas of the curriculum

The importance of art work in relation to the rest of the curriculum needs to be far more generally recognised. Understanding maths and related subjects can be greatly assisted through discoveries made in the art class, where children use repetition, balance, symmetry, division, counterchange, alternation and sequencing in their design work or pattern-making. Tessellation, dealt with in maths or history, fits equally well into an art lesson. In science, construction of hexagonal snowflake patterns will be more readily understood by children who have already experimented with patterns using rotational symmetry in art (plate 23, page vi, by Victoria at eight plus). The use of grids and trellis as a link between pattern-work and maths can be a voyage of discovery for children (plate 20, by Clare, seven plus, and plate 22, by James, eight plus, both on page vi).

The scope for picture-making increases in an exciting manner in the junior school as ideas taken from whatever work is on hand are carried out in bold and expressive ways. History subjects really live for these children through their drawings and paintings; an example is John's picture of fighting ships at the time of the Armada, done at seven plus (fig. 57). Austin, also seven plus, handles a large collage in a study of the Bedouin (plate 24, page vii).

Fig. 59 Sewing machine

Fig. 60 A typewriter

The development of drawing ability

Drawing from observation becomes well established during this year and children develop the skills to make detailed sketches. Michael's sewing machine (fig. 59), done at the age of eight plus, and Alexander's typewriter (fig. 60), at nine plus, are good examples. Imaginative drawings include more directly observed details, such as shutters and gables on houses. The typical image of a flat-fronted house with centred door and four windows, drawn by many children in the Western world, changes at about the age of six and a more three-dimensional effect begins to emerge. This indicates that a natural perception of the rules of perspective is gradually absorbed simply by seeing and drawing. Catriona's picture of a Victorian-style house (fig. 61), done at the age of eight plus, and David's aerial view of a castle with battlements (fig. 62), at nine plus, are typical of these developments.

Fig. 61 Children playing

Fig. 62 Castle and airship

Above: *Plate 17 A herd of rhinoceros*
Below left: *Plate 18 Gary's fabric design*
Below right: *Plate 19 Danielle's fabric design*

Top left: *Plate 20 Trellis pattern*
Above: *Plate 21 My brother and I*
Left: *Plate 22 Pattern based on a grid*
Below: *Plate 23 Rotational symmetry*

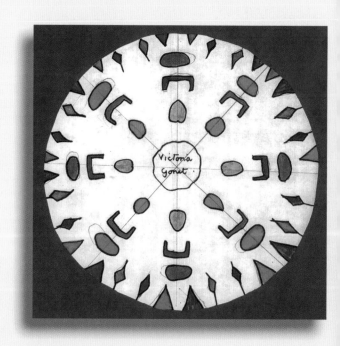

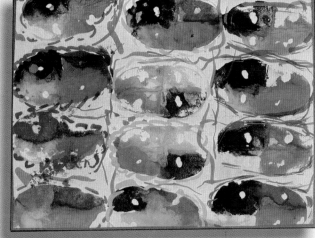

Above: Plate 24 The journey of the Magi
Right: Plate 25 A potato print
Below right: Plate 26 Stitch sampler
Below: Plate 27 A sample of weaving

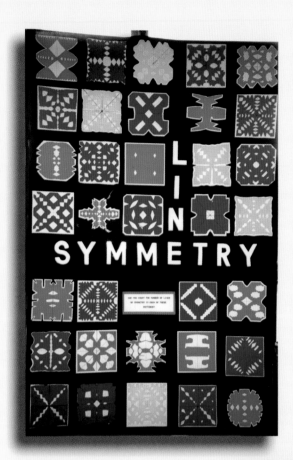

*Left: Plate 28 The teacher asks her class the simple question:
'Can you count the lines of symmetry in each of these patterns?'
Above: Plate 29 Indian elephant*

*Above: Plate 30 Giraffes racing away from danger (detail from wall panel)
Left: Plate 31 Taking a line for a walk*

Experimenting with textures

During Key Stage 2 children will develop their creativity and imagination quite naturally through the more complex activities taking place in their everyday lives, both at school and at home. All the time they are building up their skills and improving their control of materials and techniques well within the expectations of the National Curriculum. They will now experiment freely, especially with textures, and in their sketches and drawings they enjoy creating the feel of textured stone, grass, rough seas and so on. This can be seen in fig. 63, where the effect of waves crashing has been produced in a pen-and-crayon drawing of a lighthouse by John at the age of nine plus.

Fig. 63 A lighthouse and the sea

A more realistic style of expression

By the time they have reached Year 4 it is apparent from the way children express themselves in their drawings that they have moved on to a stage where they want their art work to be appreciated and understood by other people. Their visual images once expressed in a delightfully spontaneous symbolic style to satisfy their own mental vision (and making sense mostly to themselves) are now behind them, and instead they consciously attempt to use an altogether more realistic style, described as the 'analytic approach' by Margaret Morgan (*Art 4–11*, page 4).

These changes in expression are largely influenced by the child's increased perceptive understanding of the images they encounter daily in the world about them 'through their own eyes'. The continuing adjustments they make towards a greater reality at this time should be nurtured and sustained, and every help should be given in teaching them to draw well.

Fig. 64 Drawings of Tokumbo by Terrance and David

Examples of work at this stage

The studies of one of their classmates called Tokumbo Makinde, made by Terrance and David, both at the age of nine plus, demonstrate this more 'adult' approach and their work shows that they have both adjusted to new ways of 'seeing'. Terrance's sketch is rich in detail, showing Tokumbo's elaborately dressed hair, her earrings and pleated skirt. David's back view shows skilful foreshortening of her shoes, coupled with the attractive patterns on her socks. Both make interesting use of light and shade when indicating the folds and pleats in her clothes.

James uses the same approach with his realistic drawing of a saxophone made at eight years, seven months. His detail is precise, and through a skilful use of line and varying tone he brings out the shiny metallic quality of the instrument.

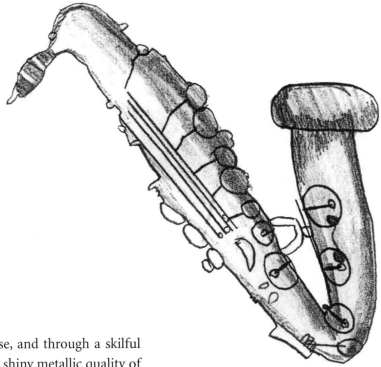

Fig. 65 Saxophone

The standard of these drawings shows these children to be working well within the expectations of Key Stage 2 in their increasing knowledge, developing skills and confident understanding and enjoyment of their art and design work.

Textiles: developing techniques in weaving and collage work

Children now have the ability to design and make up interesting blocks of weaving. By selecting materials such as string, raffia, wool, shiny ribbon, strips of dyed rag, cellophane, etc., they can create exciting contrasts in colour and texture, as shown in Kristina's colourful example in plate 27 (page vii). The children could set up a small loom, using a shoe box; later, varying sizes can be used to encourage freedom of exploration. Interesting effects can also be created by drawing out some of the threads in a loose-woven cloth and then weaving through other threads in contrasting colours and textures. Materials can be further modified by fraying the edges or knotting unravelled ends.

When weaving, they should begin to employ a broad vocabulary of terms to describe what they are doing, such as 'warp and weft', 'knotting and twisting', 'contrasting and matching'. In their collage pictures, done in a variety of fabrics, they will be making a selective use of sequins, buttons and laces and adding a wealth of embroidery stitches to their designs. They should now be able to name the stitches they use, such as cross-stitch, chain-stitch, sheaf-stitch and so on. It is helpful if each child makes a stitch sampler to refer to as their sewing techniques increase. There is an example of one of these in plate 26 (page vii).

Exploring pattern-making and print-making

A lot of experimentation with shapes and textures can be done with vegetable prints, using either a potato, a carrot or a cabbage cut through lengthways or across. Cotton reels, corks or jar lids can also be used, and children enjoy using techniques of overprinting and blending several colours. (See plate 25 on page vii.) Experiments can be made by printing from light colours to dark or by cutting parts of the block away as the pattern progresses, in what is termed a 'waste' print, until very little is left of the original block!

Fig. 66 A card stencil

A stencil made of thin card can be used as a repeating pattern. They can also be used to make greetings cards. The stencil may be used as a 'press print' and the technique developed by stencilling round the shape with a brush or sponge.

A link between art and design and maths can be seen in the experimental and adventurous approach to pattern-making shown in a Year 4 classroom display (fig. 67).

The variety of words used to describe the individual pieces of design, such as 'reflecting,

Fig. 67 Adventures in design

tessellating, contrasting, folding, exploding' indicates the children's knowledge and understanding of what they are doing. Their practical ability to carry out an interesting range of pattern work is seen in Michael's folding and tessellating and Annie's contrasting pattern, all featured in the classroom display.

Fig. 68   *tessellating*   *contrasting*   *folding*

Making a model theatre or a diorama

The imaginative picture-making which this age-group can tackle lends itself to the idea of making a simple diorama, as suggested in the National Curriculum notes. Children will enjoy drawing and planning scenes for a miniature stage, and the task of making a working model, using a simple system of concertina folds to fix the sides (see fig. 70). Melissa's underwater theme is shown in fig. 69 and this subject could well be used to make an interesting series of scenes for a diorama.

Making a model theatre will help children to develop an increasing awareness of the three-dimensional possibilities which are presented in a wide variety of subjects.

Fig. 69 Under the sea

Fig. 70 A model stage

A cross-curricular project

The children's practical work in art and design should now involve a certain amount of planning and problem solving. A project linking in with local history and the environment made a good starting point for a Year 4 class to increase their breadth of study generally, as suggested by the National Curriculum programme.

The project first involved the children working on their own to make drawings of various half-timbered Tudor houses and a church during an outing to a suitable area. They then collaborated with one another in devising a plan to scale in preparation for constructing a model village from their drawings. Next, working in groups or pairs, they constructed the models. The practical skills developed over the years in their craft work came into play as they made use of various materials, different adhesives and methods of fixing, including stapling and tacking. Their combined efforts finally came together as part of a well-integrated exercise that resulted in a worthwhile piece of art work and developed their environmental and cultural appreciation.

The project also presented an ideal opportunity to look at the art of the time. The work of Hans Holbein was viewed with considerable interest, especially the meticulous detail in his portraits of people living then and their style of dress. The very open quality of his drawings and his method of pricking the outline of them on to wooden panels prior to painting brought the subject to life for the children.

Fig. 71 Models of half-timbered houses and church:
the outcome of a cross-curricular project

Pictorial work: movement and energy

In the same way that an interest in games and athletics is now well-developed in the junior years, so the figures shown in children's drawings and paintings display vigorous movement and energy. The bold brushstrokes and textures used by Andrew for his large giraffes speeding across the landscape in a wall panel is a typical example (plate 30, page viii). The same energy of line is manifest in a lively encounter of knights jousting depicted by Paul in coloured crayon (fig. 72), and the swift movement of fighting planes climbing and descending at sharp angles, boldly expressed by David in a pen-and-ink drawing (fig. 73). All three boys were aged nine plus.

Fig. 72 Knights jousting

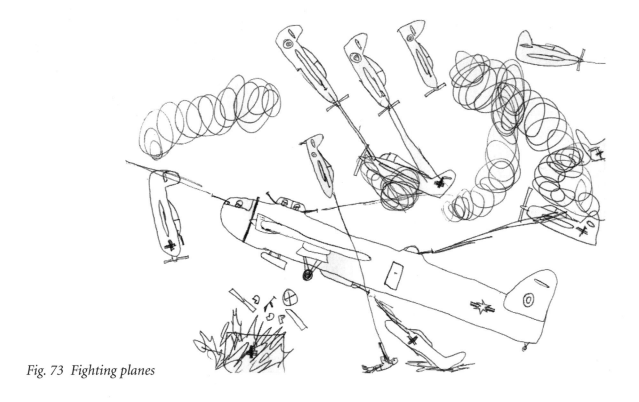

Fig. 73 Fighting planes

Using different techniques

This is the time to foster awareness and use of a range of different techniques in painting. Thickened paints can be used to show an impressionist-style build-up of texture, as used by Monet or Van Gogh; or an exercise in the use of dots of colour would explain the science of *pointillism*, evolved by Seurat. The children should now be able to compare and contrast paintings and describe the processes and methods used by different artists.

An exercise in art appreciation

In preparation for picture-making coupled with art appreciation, a mixed-age class of Years 4 and 5 looked at a set of photographs of St Lucia and each child chose a scene to paint. Having looked at the colours in the pictures of their choice, they first did some mixing, with tones and contrasting colours particularly in mind.

Before starting work, as part of their art appreciation the children looked at a landscape by Van Gogh and a scene by David Hockney. They had a discussion about the style used by these two artists, who lived and worked one hundred years apart from one another. They compared and contrasted Van Gogh's quick, 'multi-directional' brush strokes and strong use of textures and blends of colour, with Hockney's much smoother brushwork and his clear, strongly contrasting colours and deliberate use of pattern and arranged textures largely made up of regular dots. The children then made decisions about using some of these techniques in their own paintings.

Above: *Plate 32 Sunset in Castries*
Below: *Plate 33 Castries Harbour*

Above: Plate 34 Snake
Below: Plate 35 A clown

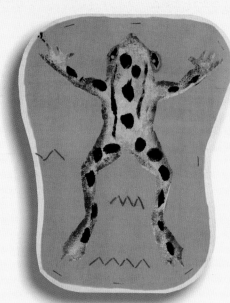

Above: Plate 36 Frog
Below: Plate 37 A bird design

Above: Plate 39 A fierce tiger
Right: Plate 40 Basket of fruit

Right: *Plate 41*
A display of work on the theme of the Vikings

Below: *Plate 42*
A secret imaginary world – children's visual images of coloured marbles

Left and right:
Plate 43 Two examples of display notices

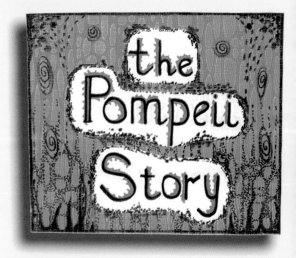

In plate 32 (page ix), Michael's dramatic painting called 'Sunset in Castries', which he made at the age of eight years eleven months, captures in the sky the tremendous warmth of colour used by Van Gogh, and at the same time the reflections on the sea mimic the artist's remarkable use of texture and movement in his paintings.

Daniel's painting, done at eight years seven months, looks very different. He employs Hockney's fresh, clear colours in his 'Castries Harbour' (plate 33, page ix) and makes use of the artist's regular-patterned textures and contrasting colours for the town and distant hills in the background. The picture has a smooth clarity about it that is far calmer than those paintings in the class influenced by Van Gogh!

From these paintings it can be seen that the children gained considerably by looking at the work of the two artists. The strategy used by the teacher to give the children a wide range of varying subjects to choose from guarded against the tendency of simply copying the artist's picture. Instead they learnt from the artists' characteristic techniques in both style and colour.

The opportunity of mixing special colours with the work of each artist in mind meant that the children were well prepared to meet the exciting challenge presented to them. The final results showed that they undoubtedly made a leap ahead of themselves on this occasion, as this experience took them forward towards their next stage of development as young artists.

Teaching drawing techniques

To promote the necessary skills, opportunity should be made for teaching children straightforward techniques during representational drawing sessions. In her sketch of some groceries, Marika at ten years eight months, learns how these different objects relate to one another as a group. She has given them solidity by shading round the different shapes in darker and lighter tones. She finds this can be done by using heavier or finer pencil lines to complete her drawing.

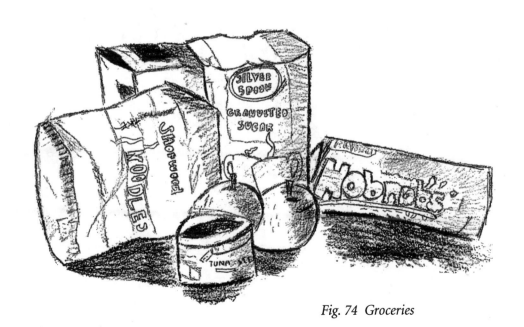

Fig. 74 Groceries

Working from observation

Throughout the years in the junior school encouragement should be given to children to continue making drawings and sketches from first-hand observation. The line drawing of a motorbike made by Mark at the age of nine plus shows the value of making use of a sketchbook out of doors whenever possible.

Kelly made a closely observed drawing of a garden snail, using a variety of tones and textures, for a class project entitled *The Environmental Garden*. She ably expressed the contrast between the smooth spiral-shaped shell and the forward movement of the muscular body. The eye and tentacles are very realistically observed. She was able to make this remarkable study of a snail with the help of a magnifying glass, and comfortably filled the area of her A4 page! Here we have an example of use being made of drawing ability in general project work, something that can be taken right across the curriculum. Kelly was nine years seven months at the time.

Art and science

A study of minibeasts forms part of the work in science in the National Curriculum programme from Year 2 onwards in the primary years. The ability of children to draw things of interest in the world about them is already developing. At the age of nine plus, John made this detailed study of a wasp in his sketchbook at home in his own time.

Fig. 75 Motorbike on stand

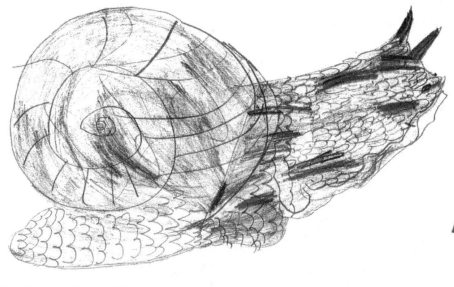

Fig. 76 A garden snail

Fig. 77 A wasp

Pattern design and print-making

By now the children's technical skills can be used to create print-blocks, with the use of string twisted round and glued on wood to form experimental star or twirl patterns, as in fig. 78. Through museum visits and the use of visual aids, children can begin to appreciate the varying design styles in textiles from other countries and they can compare these with their own work. Adventurous, experimental colour effects can be achieved through the use of marbling, wax-resist, paste-combing, etc. Simple ways of printing on fabric can be explored using a straightforward stencil method and free brushwork enhanced with additional stitching, such as the example in plate 29 (page viii).

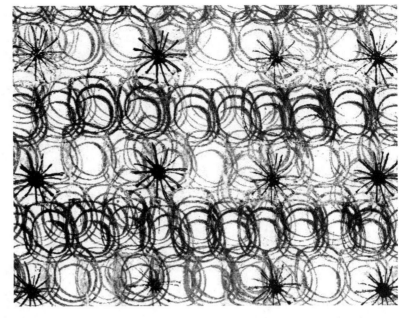

Fig. 78 String pattern

Free range can be given to these young artists' dexterity by encouraging them to explore shapes freely in much the same way as they did in the infant years by 'taking a line for a walk'. But we are now working on a very different level of course and this exercise now results in strong, vibrant, colourful pattern work (plate 31, page viii).

Puppetry in cross-curricular work

The skills of this age group can also be directed into making jointed shadow or rod puppets. A good opportunity for using these as part of drama work would be in a school assembly or an end-of-term show for parents. Ideas can perhaps be developed as part of a history project, which will lend itself to a cross-curricular study involving different characters and costumes, with the children planning and writing the story.

Fig. 79 A marionette and control

The teacher's drawing in fig. 79 shows how to make a simple marionette and control mechanism. The snake's head is made from strengthened card and the body from a plasticine roll covered with papier mâché, which is then sliced through and threaded together again. This is a good exercise in problem-solving and getting things to work.

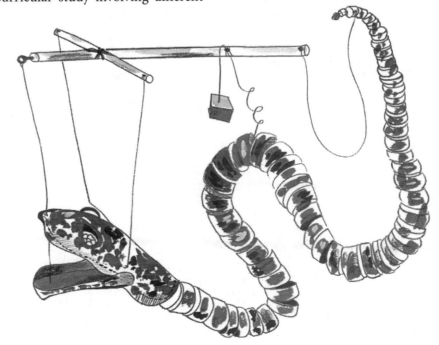

A growing awareness of reality

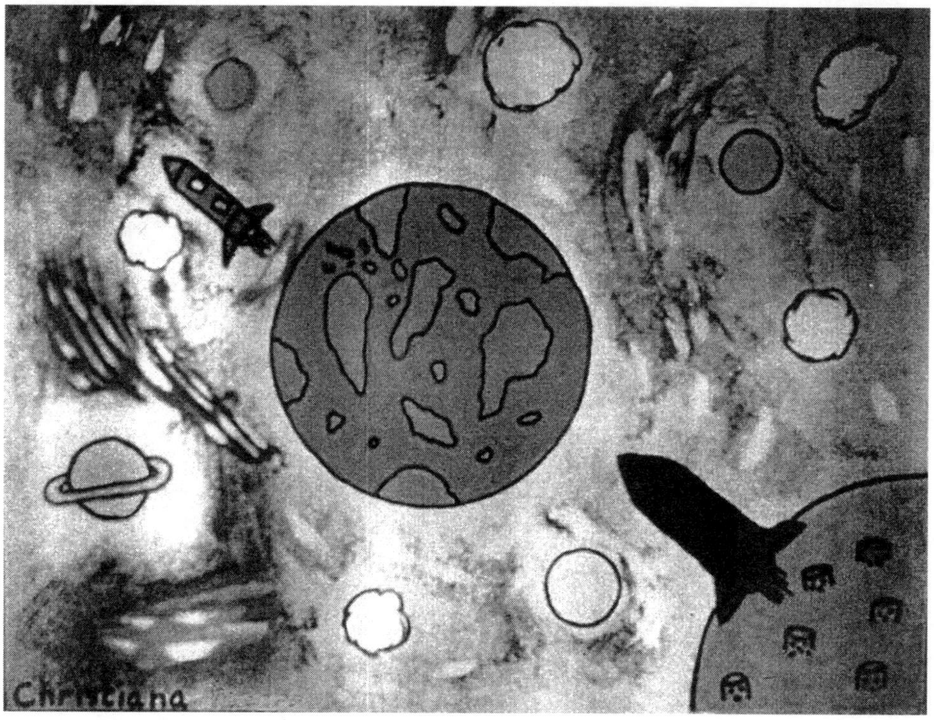

A growing interest in newsworthy events and a developing appreciation of what is happening in the world are dramatically displayed by Christiana, at the age of nine plus, in her convincing portrayal of rockets travelling in outer space (fig. 80). Her work is in line with the expectations in art and design at Key Stage 2 as she employs a range of techniques to denote conditions in outer space and the movement of the rockets. She makes use of bold line, interesting textures and contrasting tones and colours. The development in style reached by children who study such techniques used by adult artists is borne out by the following observation:

'By the time children are in Year 3 to Year 6 they enjoy investigating the different methods that have been used by artists in the past and today, producing their own interpretations of the works, and of the styles and techniques.' (Janet Graham and Heather Jeffs, *Teaching Art within the National Curriculum*, page 101)

A more mature outlook and a developing awareness of life around her are seen in Catriona's drawing of her sister and herself (fig. 81). At ten plus her style has moved towards a more realistic type of expression with a bold clarity about it. Her imaginative drawing shows her interest in clothes and also indicates her close relationship with her small sister.

Victoria's crayoned portrait of Valentina shows a clarity of line coupled with an effective use of tone and texture used for the hair and woollen jumper. In this drawing of her friend, made at the age of ten plus, her vision is very much towards the portrayal of realism and her efforts lie in this direction.

Fig. 80 *Rockets travelling to the moon*

Fig. 81 *The sisters*

Fig. 82 *Victoria's portrait of Valentina*

Learning about perspective

When considering perspective, children will benefit by looking at Hobbema's well-known painting of an avenue of tall trees narrowing away into the distance. An exercise in 'measuring' can be devised by the teacher to demonstrate 'above and below eye levels' and 'vanishing points', using drawings of block shapes. Once the rules begin to be understood children will enjoy applying their new knowledge in their own pictures. At ten years six months, Selcuk shows he has a good grasp of the subject in his drawing of a house with interesting surrounding detail.

Development in style and understanding at Key Stage 2

During Key Stage 2 pupils are expected to develop their creativity and imagination 'through more complex activities'. Here we see examples of children making a positive effort to increase their skills. For instance, Victoria appears to be leaving behind her childlike expressions in her lifelike portrait of Valentina. At the same time, the ability to use fine water-colour techniques, at nine plus, is sensitively displayed in Alison's underwater scene of a sunken wreck (fig. 84). Having carefully drawn and painted the galleon, she uses a transparent wash over it to create the underwater effect. The picture was painted as part of her history project in connection with the English navy defeating the Spanish Armada.

Both these examples, and the others throughout Year 5, show the pupils to be working well within the expected standards of the National Curriculum Programme of Study in Art and Design. The stipulation is that to extend their knowledge and understanding children should be taught about the use of colour, pattern and texture, line and tone, shape, form and space, and should use this knowledge to represent their ideas and feelings.

Their work also shows that they are recording both from experience and from imagination and making use of sketchbooks to help in exploring and developing their ideas. Their interest, enjoyment and obvious enthusiasm for the subject reveal all this.

Fig. 83 *House and garden*

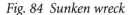

Fig. 84 *Sunken wreck*

YEAR 6

Consolidation and strengthening of skills

Fig. 85 Horrors of war

In Year 6 children are working at a steadier pace and in these top junior years they should be consolidating and strengthening the skills acquired in their art and design work. In the final year of junior school their art work should reflect the more mature attitude that might be discerned in their poems or essays. As their written descriptions become more vital and portray deeper thoughts and feelings, so their drawings and paintings can capture the same emotions. 'Horrors of war', for instance, carried out in pen-and-ink and wash by John is a typical example (fig. 85), while Moira captures a different mood by making use of line and colour in her pastel drawing to express the hidden pathos shown on a clown's face (plate 35, page x).

Art clubs

As the time devoted to various activities is now extended, lunchtime and after-school clubs prove their worth for the valuable extra working time they offer. Caroline's drawing of her shoe was done at age ten as an art club activity.

Artists' techniques: the drawings of Van Gogh

With secondary education now in view, it is helpful for children to examine the various drawing techniques employed by adult artists and to relate some of these techniques to the development of their own style. The drawing focused on here came from Van Gogh's interpretation of a sketch originally made by Rembrandt!

At the outset of his life as an artist, Vincent Van Gogh made studies of the drawings of other artists. Although most popularly known as a painter, he was also a fine draughtsman and worked in both pencil and pen. As well as his portraits, he drew a variety of subjects, including animals, trees, birds and insects, and made fine studies of buildings as well.

At ten-and-a-half Lorna has made a convincing study of Van Gogh's drawing of an elephant, in which she has paid particular attention to

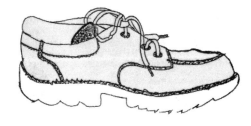

Fig. 86 My own shoe

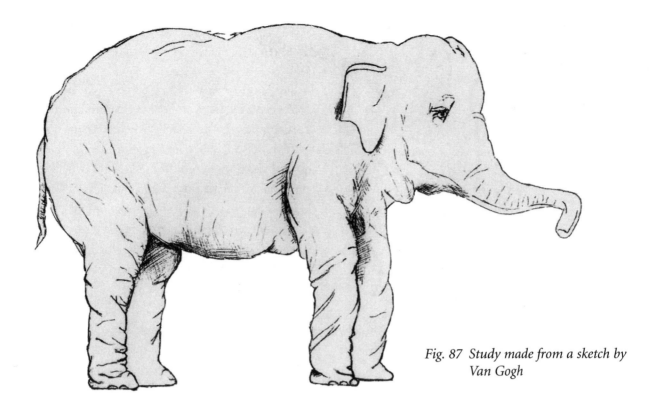

Fig. 87 *Study made from a sketch by Van Gogh*

Fig. 88 *Still life*

the cross-hatched shading and the bolder lines expressing the heavy folds in the animal's skin. Here we have an example of a young person leaping beyond her own boundaries towards the promise of a more mature expression in her art work for the future.

Drawing techniques

At ten years eight months, Corinne uses her drawing skills to make a study of three bottles, all differing in shape and size. The tallest is made of shiny dark glass. Interesting images show through the transparency of the middle-sized one, now empty, and the handle and lid on the small vinegar bottle standing in front distinguish it from the other two. The metal stopper on the tall bottle is drawn realistically and a glossy metallic paper is wrapped round the neck of the right-hand bottle. The shadows cast by the bottles complete the picture, bringing them together as a group. Their varied outline makes an arresting shape as an overall design.

Studying the work of an artist: Picasso's *Guernica*

In line with the end of Key Stage 2 requirements, the children were asked to use a combination of their creative and practical skills when making a study of Pablo Picasso's wall painting entitled *Guernica*. After initial discussions about the message the artist's painting conveyed to them, they made a series of sketches in their notebooks, choosing the portions of the picture that interested them most. The sketches they made convey the ideas of shock and horror in the images in Picasso's mural and they shaded their drawings in varying tones to accentuate the meaning.

Fig. 89 Sketches by Year 6 for Guernica

The children then enlarged one of their sketches to make their own paintings. The idea foremost in their minds was to capture the same emotions as Picasso portrayed in his picture, which revealed the horrors of civilian bombing in the village of Guernica. Further discussion ensued as to how they should tackle their paintings. The teacher limited them to the use of black and white and intermediate tones of grey in order to match Picasso's use of colour and to enable them to explore the simple use of tone to give a dramatic effect. This technique is employed to effect by Natasha in her painting, shown in fig. 90, made from the sketch alongside.

The children's sketches and the classroom display that resulted from their work show that Pablo Picasso's *Guernica* made a profound impression on the class. They have certainly understood its message and the subject has captured their interest and stirred their imagination. They also gained new experience from the discipline of making limited use of colour and added tone in their paintings.

Fig. 90 Natasha's sketch and finished painting

The way an artist works: L. S. Lowry

Fig. 91 The classroom display based on Guernica

At this age pupils should begin to be able to analyse the methods and systems used by artists in their works of art. After looking at a painting they might join together in groups to discuss it, using a brainstorming session to try to seek out some of the main features in a particular artist's way of working. They should consider the style and general layout of the work, the detail, how colour is used, the way in which figures are drawn and so on.

There is no doubt that pupils' pictorial work is often enriched through studying the work of other artists in this way. This is seen in a picture done by Sun Meen after her class had been looking at some of L. S. Lowry's industrial scenes.

Fig. 92 One of Sun Meen's preliminary sketches

Interpreting an artist's work

To help get her first ideas together Sun Meen made a page full of small drawings in her sketchbook, showing some industrial townscapes with figures moving about in them, all so characteristic of Lowry's work. These sketches contain good detail of both the immediate street scenes and the dreary-looking buildings in the surrounding area. At this stage she also investigated the use of dark and light tones and textures to give

Fig. 93 *The Jarrow marchers*

special emphasis to some of the buildings in relation to one another.

She then made her own painting to interpret what she saw in the artist's work, and this she called 'An industrial landscape' (plate 38, page xi). Choosing pastels to work in, she shows skill in handling flat areas of colour and using bold outlines, with the result that her picture shows considerable breadth of style and achieves a sharp, dramatic effect.

This comes about mainly because she has contrasted the strong shape of one building against another, using stark black against white. Conversely, the well-proportioned area of sky is limited to an atmospheric grey and the streets to dim shades of orange-brown. The steep perspective of the road running straight up towards the background, coupled with the effect of the threatening cloud of smoke hanging in the sky above the chimneys, somehow combine to accentuate the light from the factory windows, both far away and near. Their yellow glare in turn throws up the dark shapes of the figures moving back and forth, both in the distance and in the foreground, in strong relief.

Sun Meen must have gained a lot of knowledge and understanding of L. S. Lowry's work when she made her study of his paintings to cover the requirements of the National Curriculum programme. She successfully employed his characteristic use of areas of black and white to advantage, and showed a good understanding of his liking for a limited range of colour, which she adapted to her own use remarkably well. There is no doubt that her own work must have benefited considerably through this special study.

Co-operating on large-scale work

An opportunity was provided for 'working large' when a class of children made a study of the story of the Jarrow March, which took place during the great depression of the 1930s. In this case the story is dealt with on the lines of a newspaper report, with use made initially of photographs taken during the long march made by the unemployed men travelling from Jarrow to London.

The stark reality of the situation is captured in the children's paintings of the patched and worn-out clothing of the marchers and the grim expressions on their faces. Here is a typical example of art work successfully adding to the appreciation and understanding of a programme of general work dealing with a historical event.

The finished display put up in the classroom shows evidence of good co-operation and planning among the children, both in the choice of the characters portrayed and in the graduation in their size to give a perspective view of the men as they march forward hopefully, carrying their message to Parliament.

Recognisable drawings

Pupils should now be able to produce recognisable and convincing drawings when working from imagination or recording from life. In fig. 95 Anthony makes a drawing from the school grounds entitled 'A row of shops outside the school', and in fig. 96 Laura sketches an aeroplane during her visit to the Science Museum in South Kensington.

Increasing skill in design and execution

Design work has a well-balanced quality about it now, both in line and colour. The exotic bird in plate 37 (page x) is suited to either collage work or fabric design, and 'Snake' and 'Frog' are examples of stencil prints on cloth with the addition of simple embroidery.

Sun Meen's startling collage design (plate 39, page xi) comes from her lively interpretation of Henri Rousseau's tiger painting. To give a feeling of density to the jungle she uses cut-out grasses and foliage, first making delightful 'close-up' sketches of her tiger's stripes.

By the time pupils have reached Year 6 they are capable of making a sketch from observation and they have the ability to adapt that sketch into a working drawing for a painting or a design, or perhaps as an idea for a piece of pottery or other craftwork (see plates 34 and 36 on page x).

The picture by Lee in plate 40 (page xi), done at eleven plus, shows a well-planned stencil done in a step-by-step progression. By now pupils have the ability to anticipate some of the problems that might arise in carrying out such an exercise. Simple sketches, still-life studies or figure compositions are suitable subjects. The drawing is adapted and redone in thick crayon; certain areas are then cut away, leaving the main structure in bold outline. This is then stencilled on to black paper using several colours, resulting in a stained-glass-window effect.

Fig. 94 Marching on

Fig. 95 A row of shops outside the school

Fig. 96 An aeroplane

Drawing in detail

Very detailed pictures are often done by children at this stage, showing crowd-scenes or streets with an extensive number of buildings. Such drawings indicate an ability to organise the whole scene, while at the same time dealing with minute detail in certain sections. The concentration span is considerable. This is shown in a drawing done directly in pen by John after he had seen the film *Zulu*, at the age of 11 plus (fig. 97). The army fort (fig. 98) goes with it, showing an aerial view of the layout inside. Such studies will often be found among drawings done at home, where time allows for more detailed work.

Fig. 97 Zulu

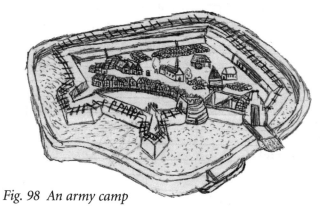

Fig. 98 An army camp

Looking ahead

Through their study of individual artists, pupils should now be familiar with an outline of the history of art. Visits to museums displaying artefacts from both their own cultural heritage and a variety of other cultures should enable them to cover the attainment targets in the National Curriculum in the course of their work. Indeed, the culmination of all their work in Art through the years should now be taking these young artists, sketchbook in hand, confidently into the future.

DISPLAYING ART WORK

> An important part of art in school includes making the whole school an attractive and aesthetically pleasing environment.
> (Janet Graham and Heather Jeffs, *Teaching Art within the National Curriculum*, page 151)

Wall displays should never be thought of simply as 'window-dressing' but rather as 'communication on a grand scale'. Their importance is that they enable children to see their own work valued and shown at its best in a changing sequence through the school year.

Classroom display

An eye-catching display of work on the Vikings is shown in plate 41 (page xii). Red backing-paper has been used to match the exciting, lively quality of the craft work done by the children. The idea of using the large Viking ship for their written work, as well as for carrying the warriors' shields, makes a contrasting use of the wall space. Interest is also sustained by the variety of objects made by the children, which are set out on the wall surrounding the ship and on the table in front of it. These include a collection of weapons, utensils and artefacts made to look like metal, wood or bone.

Fig. 99 Flight: an example of a display board

Fig. 100 shows the results of cross-curricular work, with history and art coming together in a colourful display showing the English ships defeating the Spanish Armada. While the galleons are shown fighting their battle in the scene above, the space below is cleverly used for an underwater cross-section, showing a study of marine creatures of the past done in cut-paper work. Both displays belong to Year 5.

A three-dimensional effect is captured in the fascinating work on 'Flight' (fig. 99), where science is linked with art and craft and design, and the mounted work has a quality of 'lift, movement and forward thrust' in line with the subject matter portrayed.

Staplers should not be used to 'clamp' display material to wall-boards. This approach is too permanent, because it is best if the work is changed frequently, or at least adjusted or rearranged to keep interest alive. Map pins rather than drawing pins are most suitable for pinning things up. With the use of staplers there is usually a build-up of old staples left after the display has been taken down and these leave the surface of pin-boards in an unworkable state.

Fig. 100 *The defeat of the Armada*

Teachers' display notices

As we live in a world where lettering of a wide variety of style and size can be printed out on computer, it becomes increasingly important for teachers to design their own individual handwritten notices to accompany the displays of children's work in the classrooms and about the school. Lettering is an essential part of these displays and for the most part it should be designed so that it adds something significant to the message of the display rather than simply being printed out. The examples of lettering in plate 43 (page xii) suggest the burning city of Pompeii and, in contrast, the cool and tranquil countryside of Japan.

A well-balanced approach

In the display shown in plate 42 (page xii), produced by Year 6, each child has visualised an imaginary world existing inside a coloured marble. The project is an ideal example of that desirable 'balance' between class subjects – in this case between the visual image and the written word. It would surely not be feasible to attempt to measure the importance of one activity against another, since both are valuable and neither could be described as infringing on the other.

Fig. 101 *Inside a marble*

The variety of expression and colour seen in the shapes makes a sparkling impact on the display's surroundings. It conveys the children's interest in using creative words matched by their enjoyment of making paintings. The 'circular message' inscribed by the teacher inside a marble (fig. 101) shows the slight distortion created by its roundness. Her words suggest the feast of ideas to be discovered inside this imaginary world of coloured glass.

The formation of a simple alphabet

In the junior school children should make their own slogans and notices and their approach will be helped by seeing a good standard of display about the school. For capital letters I recommend the use of a simple alphabet based on the proportions of a full square, three-quarter square and half square, so that the width of any letter is easily adjusted to its height.

At the age of seven plus, Catherine in Year 3 makes a notice suitable for a poster advertising a sale of flowers or an attractive design for a book cover. She uses capital letters which follow my suggestions of basing the proportions on a square.

Fig. 102 Catherine's lettering

Andrew, in Year 4, at the age of nine plus, uses lower-case lettering to express something dangerous. He conveys his message in an imaginative manner and the basic proportions of the letters are adhered to. He employs diminishing size in his letters to give a more sinister effect.

Fig. 103 Andrew's display work

Melissa, in Year 5, aged nine plus, has used her name as part of an exercise in perspective and discovering vanishing points. The result is quite dramatic, lending an overall feeling of solidity and a three-dimensional effect to the individual letters.

Fig. 104 Vanishing point

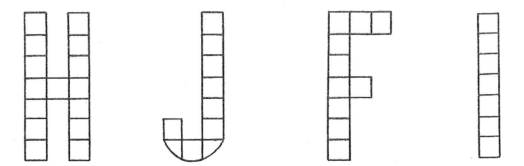

Fig. 105 Using units to build letters

The alphabet above is designed to a height of seven units. If the children are using squared paper they can conveniently adjust their block lettering to different heights and widths. The proportions of the alphabet below make a good general rule. The shape of the letters can be adapted or refined according to taste.

ABCDEFGHIJ
KKLMMMNOPQR
SSTUVWXYZA

Fig. 106 A simple block alphabet

Learning about graphic design

The use of letters can be a positive step towards understanding and appreciating the rudiments of graphic design.

Children can learn that simply by altering the size or colour of letters and emphasising the shape they are contained in, the whole meaning of words can be altered! This is where a profitable link can be made with the children's work in ICT and their natural creativity can be brought to bear on the subject.

ART APPRECIATION

As children's skills in art and design develop, so does their awareness and curiosity about works of art and craft produced by adult artists and the different methods of drawing and painting used. This growing interest should be encouraged through art appreciation. Children should start to recognise the styles belonging to individual artists and should begin to have an understanding of such terms as 'abstract', 'impressionist', 'cubist' and so on. Examples of how art appreciation can be introduced in the classroom have been included in earlier chapters.

In fig. 107 the teacher uses a simple visual aid to help her pupils see how the straightforward drawing of a chair with a guitar propped against it can be shown in different ways. The same subject is shown in fig. 108 as an abstract pattern such as might be seen in some of Picasso's work, while in fig. 109 it has turned into a surrealist study in the style of Salvador Dali. Other movements in art could be demonstrated in this way.

Fig. 107 The basic drawing

Children will discover the word 'classical' in relation to ancient Greek architecture and in art they find that the same term applies to the sculpture of Michelangelo and the paintings of Ingres. A further opportunity to explore different styles can be taken by showing them a 'classical' drawing of a pot and a flattened-out drawing of the same thing, such as the cubist artist Georges Braque might have painted.

Fig. 108 Abstract style

Fig. 109 Surrealism

Fig. 110 Classical and cubist images

Originality a priority

I want to emphasise the importance of preserving the child's own original expression throughout their art work. In order to achieve this, the teacher must be the one who opens the way for each young pupil to express themselves at their own level and in their own individual style. In other words the teacher's primary interest should be in discovering what each child has to say through the development of their own perceptions so that their progress is maintained along the right path.

The world of the child, not of the adult

Of course, classes make studies of the work of adult artists from time to time. In these cases they are looking for certain qualities in that work and at the same time they are absorbing the artistic culture of the period. But there is never any question of trying to directly copy drawings or paintings simply as a show of skill. However, sometimes an exercise might be carried out in making a special study of some aspect of an artist's drawing or painting, as in the picture based on Van Gogh's drawing in fig. 87 (page 47). This was done to further the child's own techniques, which would then be built on for future use. So in this case the child is enhancing a skill rather than simply copying for its own sake. This has always been a practice in the teaching of art.

Rob Barnes warns against the tracing of a teacher's outline or the copying of adult work rather than allowing children to make their own drawings. He mentions specifically such things as the use of colouring books (designed of course by adults), because by going along that path we no longer have the child's original interpretation of the world about them, but we have a mock adult's form of expression instead! He puts his point very succinctly in his book *Art, Design and Topic Work* (pages 41–3), saying that once an adult image is held up as the standard to be achieved, we are really saying to children, 'Your work is not good enough – stop being yourselves and do it like this'. He then asks: 'Whose interpretation of the world do we want?'

Japanese influences

The fresh colour and simplicity of line in Japanese prints influenced many nineteenth-century artists. Van Gogh sometimes made oil paintings directly from woodblock prints and Monet had a Japanese bridge built in his garden at Giverny, which can be seen in some of his paintings. The notable American James McNeill Whistler, while living in London, did several paintings in the Japanese style, even signing them in the oriental manner in the shape of a butterfly! This example shows the type of block print from which he may have derived his signature.

Studying other cultures: a Japanese exhibition

The study of non-Western art from a variety of cultures can be dealt with economically as regards time and effort if some of the work is jointly shared between classes. Exhibiting samples of the art of different countries (as well as ancient and modern civilisations) is a good way of offering children further experiences in art appreciation.

An exhibition I set up about Japan, accompanied by a talk with the use of slides given at infant and junior levels, appealed to all age groups throughout my school. It included photographs of everyday life in Japan and their traditional street festivals. There were also hand-painted ceramics, woodblock prints and dolls and a special section devoted to paper exhibits, including dragon kites, colourful streamers and examples of origami done by Japanese children. A study of an artistic culture like this, maintaining its ancient traditions in a modern world, helps to develop an appreciation of non-Western art. Children will learn about the differences and similarities between their own way of life and that of the Japanese, who live on the other side of the world.

Fig. 111 A Japanese child in school

Fig. 111 shows one of a set of slides about life in Japan: it depicts a Japanese girl in school practising writing with brush and ink. The children also learn Western-style handwriting, which is used increasingly in Japan.

ORGANISATION AND RESOURCES

If children are to carry out art and craft work in a workable environment, classrooms must take on a proper workshop atmosphere. So even if special time is allotted for drawing and painting, the paint table set up in the Nursery and Reception classes should be available also throughout the infant and junior school, either for work in progress or for children to finish off work at any time.

The painting table – Nursery level

The Nursery painting table shown in fig. 112 is organised for two children working side by side. It is a suitable height for young children to stand at their work and there is a plastic-covered screen at the back to protect walls against splashes. For this age group paintpots are best kept in a long container, both for ease of access and a straightforward choice of colours. Baked-bean-type tins are best, and if safely anchored in this way there is no danger of spills. There should be no limitations in the choice of colours, and a range of ten seems to be about the right number. The hot colours, for instance, could be yellow, vermilion, ultramarine and brown, and the cold colours, cobalt blue, green, pink and crimson, and there should also be black and white. Pencils should

Fig. 112 The painting table

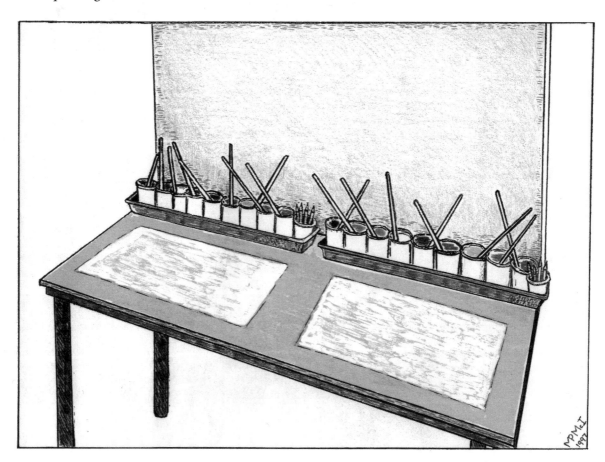

always be on hand for children to draw with if they want to. Attempts to draw first before painting will become the natural sequence of events if pencils are provided.

Adapting the junior classroom

The layout of classrooms with tables rather than desks in the infant school makes practical work easy to organise, but some system needs to be adopted in junior classes to make the room suitable for carrying out art and craft lessons. As I mentioned briefly in the chapter on Year 3, furniture can be adapted for children to work in pairs if two desks are pushed together and a light board, cut to size, placed on top, making a useful work table. The boards can easily be stored when not in use. A practical addition to this would be a folding table; this can be used to hold art or craft materials during a lesson, or it can become an extra work table to be used either in the classroom or in a corridor. It can be stowed away at the end of the lesson.

One clear necessity in every classroom is a good-sized sink. Trying to manage by carrying water from a nearby tap makes organisation very difficult. With the recent calls for the raising of standards in education, the provision of such facilities should come within the general rule for every classroom.

The use of easels

Easels are best reserved just for drawing or pastel work because paints used on the vertical tend to run down and spoil the picture. They take up a lot of space, so unless the room is large, a table with pencils, pens and crayons is preferable for drawing.

Storage

Classrooms throughout the primary school have to cater for many activities, but as few of them have built-in cupboards careful consideration needs to be given to satisfactory storage. Problems in storing painting equipment and children's large-scale work can be solved by the provision of low shelving and drawers, while a multiple-stacking unit will house a variety of tools and materials. Maintaining an attractive environment is all-important, so some equipment needs to be curtained off under shelves and worktops to keep things looking tidy.

There should be good map chests available, large enough to take A2 paper, for the storage of children's finished work and special papers. If space for this large furniture is a problem in the classroom, there may be a corner in a nearby corridor that can be used. Large chests should also be provided for a collection of visual aids, which need to be catalogued and kept in a specially designated area. If they are for general use a proper storage system needs to be devised to keep track of different sets of mounted sheets, and here I would advise colour-coding. One

Fig. 113 A storage unit

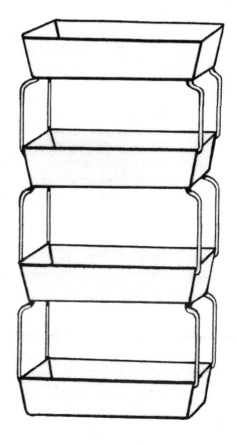

Fig. 114 *A simple design for a display screen which is approximately 1.5m high and 1.25m wide*

Fig. 115 *The resource area*

important resource is a selection of reproductions dealing with the principal schools of painting, such as the classical, impressionist, cubist and so on. These can be kept in large different-coloured folders, with the separate sheets coded to the same colour as the folder and a simple library system used to keep track of things. Slides and videos can be dealt with similarly in their own special area.

A central display area in the school

A focus of interest can be provided by creating a display area in a central position and by changing the exhibition every two or three weeks. A set of display screens for use here and elsewhere round the school will prove their worth. A collection of artefacts, such as coloured glass, dolls or toys from other countries, or a selection of wood-carvings on loan from the local museum might make a suitable display. Items collected from the time of the Second World War, as part of a project being done by one of the classes, would stimulate great interest.

The children will make very positive connections with what is being shown if their ideas are invited from time to time for displays, and they will feel more directly involved if they bring things in from home sometimes to add to the collections. Apart from being an interesting focal point, such arrangements encourage young people to observe, enquire, respond and evaluate, and relate more fully to the world around them, in line with the programmes of work for the National Curriculum.

Display screens, such as the one shown here, can be used either individually or joined up in rows in large areas such as the school hall. Work can of course be pinned on both sides. Interesting colour schemes can be introduced, depending on the particular use being made of the screens at the time. The boards can easily be recoated with emulsion paint when colours need to be refreshed or changed.

The resource area or 'museum'

If room is available, there should be shelf space allocated for collections of objects for general use in the school. These objects can be attractively set out and used as source materials to stimulate and develop ideas. The resource area should contain sets of objects such as interesting bottles, pots and vases, pebbles, shells, fir-cones and seed-cases, small toys such as trains, carts, boats and cranes, and attractive cloths and drapes or things of distinctive character such as a pair of old boots or shoes.

Fig. 116 Copper vase in the style of Van Gogh

Such an area is not only a great back-up for work from observation and imagination, but it can also double as the school museum and will thus provide exhibits from time to time for the central display area. In this way opportunities will present themselves for the teacher to guide children to recognise what is well designed or aesthetically attractive and to express their opinions about some of the items in the collection. The descriptions pupils give in a class discussion might express their ideas about, for instance, shiny surfaces, strong patterns, contrasting colours or the fact that something is slender or solid in design. Pupils might also consider whether an object is old-fashioned, if it would be useful, and finally whether they like it or not!

Displaying artists' work

Good framed reproductions around the school help with art appreciation. It is a good policy to change them round from time to time or sometimes pick out a particular one for special display and follow this up with discussions about the artist's style. The children should be encouraged to observe how some of the objects in famous paintings compare with those in the school collection. An example might be the copper vase painted by Van Gogh in his painting *Fritillarias*, dated 1887. This will open up another area of investigation into the work of adult artists. By drawing and painting a variety of such objects the children will expand their ideas and gain some new experiences in the world of art.

VISITS TO GALLERIES AND MUSEUMS

Museum visits have always played an important part in the life of schools. But since they have become a part of the programmes of study in the National Curriculum, in which children work from source material collected in galleries and museums from different cultures and times, an even more productive element has been introduced in this field.

The museum visit

In her book *Learning out of school* (page 32) Molly Harrison, a former curator of the Geffrye Museum, asks the important question: 'What can they do when they get there?' She gives a very clear reply:

'Obviously we want them to look, to look with real interest and enjoyment, with real delight and with some measure of understanding. And we want them to question, both verbally and in their own minds, to build upon what they have seen and to ask about anything that occurs during their visit.'

So it should be part of the young visitors' training to be appreciative of what is being offered to them at the museum.

Careful selection needs to be exercised about what they should do during their time there so that the mistake is not made of rushing round and attempting too much on any one occasion, in which case their interest would become superficial and not lead to any real aesthetic or intellectual appreciation. Whereas a class properly equipped with sketching materials, and split up into manageable groups in the care of helpful adults to give guidance (and time checks), should achieve something really worthwhile.

Practical considerations

A certain amount of preparation has to be made by the teacher to ensure the visit will be a success. It is a help if the children have some idea of what to expect when they get to the museum if they have not been before. Some places have trained staff who will explain any rules that need to be observed and who might also show the group round on arrival and explain the exhibits. Some museums provide equipment for drawing, such as stools, cushions or sketching boards. Drawing is one of the most satisfying means of recording a visual experience, and if the children add a few brief explanatory notes to their sketches these can be very helpful for future reference. Fig. 117 shows some interesting observations made by Thomas at the age of ten on his drawing, while Steven's majestic eagle, done in the Natural History Museum as part of a project on flight, almost speaks for itself (fig. 118).

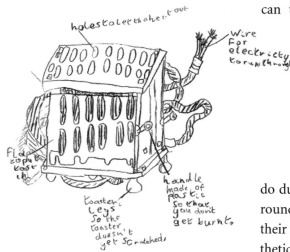

Fig. 117 Drawing of an early electric toaster

Fig. 118 An eagle

Handling exhibits

Children enjoy handling exhibits. In this way they become familiar with an object and the materials it is made of, its shape and texture. They gain from running their fingers over a woodcarving or working a spinning wheel. If the museum goes so far as to put boys' and girls' historical costumes (with the added use of swords, hats, fans, etc.) at the disposal of groups, the subject comes alive and makes a really lasting impression.

Fig. 119 Flask in the form of a dolphin leaping over the waves

Gaining from the experience: follow-up work

Many museums issue a series of subject folders containing prints and questionnaires which can be used in a variety of ways. These form a valuable source of information and are particularly helpful in enabling children to expand their knowledge of worldwide cultures and to learn more about their own land. Children can also do a wide range of art and craft work in connection with their visits, perhaps by making costume puppets and masks or by creating collages and experimenting with printing on cloth. They could also make and decorate pots and bowls and make sketches or models of some of the things they have seen.

Sketching in the museum

These line drawings (figs 119–21), accompanied by clear notes and colour descriptions, were done in his sketchbook by Richard, at eleven plus, when visiting the Greek and Roman antiquities in the British Museum.

Fig. 120 A juttus bottle

The principal civilisations and our own culture

The school's collection of visual aids should cover aspects of the principal civilisations from earliest times, including information on Egyptian pyramids and temples, Roman towns and temples and an overall study of the Roman army. Cultural material on Britain should deal with Gothic cathedrals, stained-glass windows, illuminated manuscripts, Norman castles, medieval architecture and developing styles up to the present day. Ceramics, textiles, paintings, dress, furniture, etc. are all part of the same study.

The British Museum covers a great deal of this material in its departments of Egyptian, Greek and Roman Antiquities and British and Medieval Antiquities. Local museums also exhibit a considerable amount, though naturally on a smaller scale. The shops in our national museums and galleries are a rich source of visual aids. Reproductions of paintings and artefacts and educational books and resources dealing with special themes, particularly world cultures, are always worth investigating.

The National Gallery Education Department

The National Gallery Education Department has some excellent work programmes relating to its collections of works of art. These include talks for pupils from the ages of three upwards, tailor-made to schools' requirements. Courses are provided for both primary and secondary teachers and for parents and children.

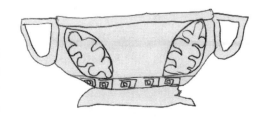

Fig. 121 A podanipter foot-bath

*Fig. 122 An angel. Girl aged 5+. This drawing was done by Hannah during a family drawing event 'Angles on Angels' held at the National Gallery. The inspiration was **The Coronation of the Virgin** by Jacabo di Cione.*

Local museums and galleries

In recent years successful efforts have been made throughout the UK for many local museums and galleries to reach their full potential. With local authority grants many have been refurbished, and as well as their permanent displays, they offer frequently changing temporary exhibitions. Although most museums are to be found in larger towns and cities, there are many smaller ones, often with fascinating exhibits, in rural areas. Information about all these can be found on the internet and weekend and holiday visits are especially welcomed, with parent participation increasingly encouraged.

Directories and guides

There are a number of directories and guides available, such as *The Cambridge Guide to the Museums of Britain and Northern Ireland* by Ann Nicholls and Kenneth Hudson and *The Blue Guide to Museums and Galleries of London* by Malcolm Rogers. Teachers would do well to find out about local guides. *Schools Out: A teacher's guide to museums in Surrey* is an excellent one in this respect: it has a detailed A to Z of all the museums in the county and is full of information to enable teachers to make the most of the facilities offered.

Selected galleries and museums

(a) London area
Schools in and around London have an excellent choice of galleries and museums to visit. These are just some of them:

Bethnal Green Museum of Childhood
British Museum
The Commonwealth Institute
Dulwich Picture Gallery
Geffrye Museum
Horniman Museum
Museum of London
National Gallery
National Maritime Museum, Greenwich
National Portrait Gallery
Tate Gallery and Tate Modern
Wallace Collection
Whitechapel Art Gallery
Victoria and Albert Museum

*Fig. 123 Horse and rider. Girl aged 5+. This drawing was done by Saskia during a family workshop 'A little light relief' held at the National Gallery. It was inspired by **The vision of St Eustace** by Antonio Pisanello.*

(b) Other parts of Britain and Ireland
The capital cities all have good museums. In addition, regional museums are of increasing value these days, both for their permanent exhibits and for occasional displays of fine art exhibits organised by

local groups. Many have lending systems arranged in conjunction with local education authorities, whereby boxes of exhibits are sent out to schools in the area. Some will arrange a special programme to link up with any particular topic the children are working on. Many have specialist exhibits.

Edinburgh: The Museum of Childhood – children's books, toys and games, displays relating to the health, upbringing, education and dress of children

Cardiff: National Museum of Wales, Cathays Park – emphasis on the story of Wales from the earliest times, with machines relating to older industries, also a mining gallery

Dublin: National Museum of Ireland – archaeological section including prehistoric gold and early Christian metalwork, Viking material, decorative art of Japan and China

The American Museum, Claverton Manor, Bath – folk art and the American Indian (Boxes sent out to schools)

The Kingston Museum and Art Gallery, Kingston-upon-Thames – the story of Kingston from its ancient origins to the present day through permanent and changing displays

Leicester Museum and Art Gallery – British and foreign natural history, palaeontology (including articulated dinosaur), English and European art from sixteenth century to the present day (Boxes sent out to schools)

The Royal Albert Memorial Museum, Exeter – work by local artists and a children's gallery that mounts a series of special exhibitions throughout the year

York Castle Museum, York – a costume collection, a reconstruction of an old York street with genuine Victorian shop fronts, displays of armour, weapons and swords

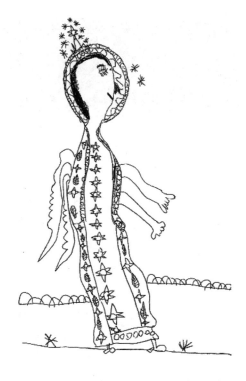

Fig. 124 An angel with stars. Girl: aged 5+. Saskia's drawing, taken from the 'Angles on Angels' event held at the National Gallery. The inspiration was **The Coronation of the Virgin** *by Jacabo di Cione.*

TEACHERS' ART AND CRAFT NOTEBOOKS

I suggest that teachers make art and craft notebooks for themselves in which to record brief notes about ways of tackling particular crafts, the materials used and how the children managed them to their best advantage. Below is a list of types of craft work suitable for the primary years which might be included in your notebook.

(a) Paper

Collage, using lentils and pasta shapes on paper
Rubbings made from tree bark, leaves, brickwork, etc.
Stencils made from card
Paper stars
Using pressed flowers in craft and design
Paper windmills
Paste-combing, exploring the use of different combs and colour mixes
Paper-weaving, using textured papers in contrasting colours

(b) Textiles

Decorative textile panels, exploring a variety of fabrics and threads
Sewing soft toys
Stitching a sampler, using basic embroidery stitches
Weaving with simple looms, stitching and knotting various threads and fibres
Tie-and-dye, knotting, pegging and tying
Stencil-printing on paper and cloth with sponge and brush
Batik, brushing, painting, dripping, stamping and crazing
Simple screen-printing
Marbling

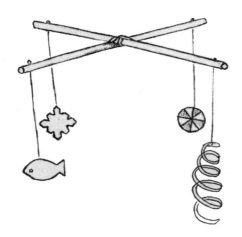

(c) Form and three-dimensions

Puppets, including finger puppets, glove puppets and rod puppets
Making mobiles in various sizes
Model-making with junk material, boxes, etc.
Designing jumping-jacks
Spinning tops and whizzer tops, exploring patterns and colours
Making and flying kites and windsocks
Mask-making, clowns, animals, etc.
Papier mâché, various uses

Keeping a scrapbook

Keep a scrapbook of photographs, examples of children's work and the teacher's sketches of details of class work. This will offer a visual aid to show children how things have been done previously and how to plan ahead.

Ideas for craft work

Fun with card and papier mâché

Papier mâché was used to make the head of the clown opposite, which was then fixed on a light spring to make a balancing toy. Mobiles cut out of card make good decorations and spinning tops provide another opportunity for mathematical designs. The teacher should note here that a pencil sharpener will provide the necessary point on the end of the dowel rod!

Masks and animal shapes

Masks of different kinds of animals can be made by using simple techniques with folded and cut-out card. Masks and head-dresses can be similarly devised on a larger scale for use in plays and school assemblies. This type of work draws the children's attention to 'profiling' and it links in naturally with maths in providing an exercise both in symmetry and in the three-dimensional aspect of objects.

Jumping jacks

Jumping jacks can be made up into a variety of characters made to jump with strings. They are fixed with paper fasteners and are equally effective either mounted on card or used as part of a larger group on a decorative wall panel. The children can start by making themselves a folder with step-by-step instructions for this craft.

Modelling

Modelling work with clay, using different shapes such as duck, fish, snail or ladybird, can be extended by decorating with slip, then glazing and firing. Air-hardening materials, which do not require firing, can be used instead. Alternatively, papier mâché can be moulded over a simple plasticine shape, then brightly painted after fine sandpapering and finished by polishing with ordinary clear furniture polish or varnish.

Weaving

Weaving can be taken a step further with the use of textured papers. Instead of using two plain-coloured papers, children can experiment with papers in two predominately different colours that they have previously crayoned and given a colour wash to produce a stippled effect, before ruling, cutting and weaving. A loosely woven cotton floor cloth opens up possibilities as use can be made of ribbons and threads to weave through the coarse warp and weft.

Textiles

Borrowing from their previous experience, the children should carry out their textile work with increasing skill and enjoyment in the use of both free and traditional stitching. This is shown in Alison's collage work of spider and ladybird, done at the age of five plus, where she displays an interest in using a variety of threads and stitches.

BIBLIOGRAPHY

Barnes, Rob, *Art, Design and Topic Work 8–13*. London: Unwin-Hyman, 1987.

Barnes, Rob, *Teaching Art to Young Children 4–9*. London: Unwin-Hyman, 1987.

Bernard, Bruce, *Van Gogh*. London: Dorling Kindersley, 1992.

Van Breda, A., *Pleasure with Paper*. Whitstable: Latimer Trend & Co. Ltd, 1972.

Civardi, Anne and Thomson, Ruth, *Family Fun in the National Gallery*. London: National Gallery Ltd, 2001.

Clement, Robert, *The Art Teacher's Handbook*. Cheltenham: Stanley Thornes, 1993.

Cox, Maureen, *Children's Drawings*. Harmondsworth: Penguin Books, 1992.

Cox, Maureen, *Children's Drawings of the Human Figure*. Hove, UK, and Hillside, USA: Lawrence Erlbaum, 1993.

Cox, Maureen, *Drawings of People by the Under-5s*. UK and USA: The Falmer Press, 1997.

Department for Education and Employment, *All Our Futures: Creativity, Culture & Education*. National Advisory Committee on Creative and Cultural Education, 1999.

Drake, Jane, *Planning Children's Play and Learning in Foundation Stage*. London: David Fulton, 2000.

Eisner, Elliot W., *Cognition and the Curriculum*. New York and London: Longman, 1982.

Fineberg, Jonathan, *The Innocent Eye: Children's Art and the Modern Artist*. USA: Princeton University Press, 1997.

Fitzsimmons, Su, *Start With Art*. Hemel Hempstead: Simon and Schuster Education, 1994.

Gentle, Keith, *Teaching Painting in the Primary School*. London: Cassell, 1993.

Graham, Janet and Jeffs, Heather, *Teaching Art within the National Curriculum*. Leamington Spa: Scholastic, 1993.

Haines, Susanne, *Papier Mâché*. London: Charles Letts, 1990.

Harrison, Molly, *Learning out of school. A teacher's guide to the educational use of museums*. London: Ward Lock Educational, 1970.

Holmes, Saira, *Schools Out. A Teacher's Guide to Museums in Surrey*. Surrey Museums Consultative Committee, 1999.

Hudson, Kenneth and Nicholls, Ann, editors, *The Cambridge Guide to the Museums of Britain and Ireland*. Cambridge University Press, 1989.

Micklethwaite, Lucy, *I Spy Numbers in Art*. London: Collins, 1992.

Morgan, Margaret, *Art 4–11: Art in the early Years of Schooling*. In association with Suffolk County Council, Stanley Thornes, 1988.

Owen, Cheryl, *Paper Crafts*. London: Salamander Books, 1991.

Penrose, Roland, *Picasso*. London: Phaidon, 1991

Read, Herbert, *Education Through Art*. Hertford: The Shenval Press, 1949.

Richardson, Joy, *Looking at Pictures*. London: A. & C. Black/ National Gallery Ltd, 2001.

Richardson, Marion, *Writing and Writing Patterns*. University of London Press, 1935.

Rogers, Malcolm, *The Blue Guide to Museums and Galleries of London*, 1991

Rowe, Gaelene, *Guiding Young Artists*. Melbourne: Oxford University Press, 1987.

Schaffner, Ingrid, *Pablo Picasso*. New York: The Wonderland Press, 1998.

Seville, Renee, *Beginning Arts and Crafts*. London: Evans Brothers, 1970.

Watt, Fiona, *The Usborne Book of Art Ideas*. London: Usborne Publishing, 2001.

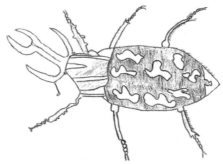

Fig. 125 A horned beetle

INDEX